HIGH-FIBER WHOLESOME RECIPES

20g+ Fiber And 20g+ Protein In Every Meal

Copyright ©2024 by Krupa and Krish

All rights reserved. No part of this publication may be reproduced, distributed, or transmitted in any form or by any means, including photocopying, recording, or other electronic or mechanical methods, without the prior written permission of the publisher, except in the case of brief quotations embodied in critical reviews and certain other noncommercial uses permitted by copyright law.

Disclaimer:

The recipes and information provided in this book are intended for informational purposes only. They are not meant to be a substitute for advice from a professional healthcare provider. The dietary information and health tips provided are not intended to diagnose, treat, cure, or prevent any disease or health condition.

Before making any changes to your diet or nutrition plan, it is advised that you consult with a healthcare professional, especially if you have specific health conditions or dietary needs. The author and publisher of this book disclaim any liability for adverse effects directly or indirectly resulting from the use or application of any of the recipes or information contained herein.

The nutritional information provided for each recipe is an estimate and may vary based on the specific ingredients used and portion sizes. For precise nutritional guidance, consulting with a registered dietitian or nutritionist is recommended.

By using this book, you acknowledge and agree that neither the author nor the publisher shall be liable for any loss, damage, or health issues that may arise from the use of the recipes or information provided.

ABOUT THE AUTHORS

Krupa and Krish is a remarkable mother and son-duo initiated by their shared passion for promoting a healthy lifestyle through their creative endeavors. Together, they have embarked on a mission to inspire and educate others on the importance of holistic well-being. They strive to accomplish this goal by travelling the world to learn about different cultures, lifestyles, and views, cooking together to not only reinforce their knowledge, but also their relationship, and finally, exploring various topics such as, culinary arts, financial management, and self-improvement. They plan to use this knowledge in an attempt to expand the boundaries of traditional wisdom and modern living.

Krupa is a multi-talented individual with a diverse skill set. As a Certified Health Coach who is passionate about healthy lifestyle, she brings an abundance of knowledge and expertise to the culinary world. Her dedication to promoting healthy living goes beyond dietary choices; she firmly believes that a healthy lifestyle encompasses all aspects of one's life. Krupa has honed her talents as a Fashion Designer and a Creative Content Creator, granting her the skills to craft engaging and visually appealing material that resonates with her audience. Her unique ability to blend traditional and ancient wisdom on topics like healthy living, personal finance, and contemporary lifestyle requirements has been a driving force behind the creation of their books.

Krupa's deep-rooted passion for encouraging on going personal growth is reflected within her work. She is committed to making wellness and longevity accessible to all. She has channeled her creative energies into producing books, articles and content that are informative, easy to understand, and implement in daily life.

Krish, the youngster in this dynamic duo, is a teenager with an incredible eye for detail. His keen eye and unwavering commitment to excellence are key factors in the success of KRKR Books. Despite his age, Krish has proven to be an incredibly valuable asset in their mission to promote a healthier world. His fresh perspective and observation skills polish up their projects, ensuring they remain relevant and relatable to the younger generation.

Together, Krupa and Krish have founded KRKR Books, a brand dedicated to spreading their message of well-being and Personal growth. Through their collaborative efforts, they have crafted books and resources that empower individuals of all ages to embark on a healthier and happier lifestyle. Their unique blend of talents and enthusiasm makes them an incredible team in wellness and personal development literature.

The journey of Krupa and Krish is an inspiring example of the power of family, collaboration, and a shared vision. Their dedication to the cause of promoting healthy living is an invitation for readers to join them on a path to better, happier, and healthier life. As they continue to create insightful content, it is clear that Krupa and Krish are doing their best to make a lasting impact on the body, the only real home a person has, one page at a time.

INTRODUCTION

Welcome to "High-Fiber Wholesome Recipes," a cookbook designed to help you embrace a healthier and more wholesome way of eating. Fiber is an essential component of a balanced diet, and this collection of recipes is dedicated to helping you incorporate it into your daily meals without sacrificing taste or satisfaction.

In today's fast-paced world, it's easy to overlook the importance of fiber in our diets. With the prevalence of processed foods and busy lifestyles, we often opt for convenience over nutrition. This cookbook aims to change that by offering a wide array of delicious, fiber-rich recipes that are not only good for your body but also tantalizing for your taste buds.

The Importance of Fiber

Fiber is nature's gift to our digestive system. It aids in digestion, helps maintain a healthy weight, and plays a crucial role in reducing the risk of chronic diseases, such as heart disease, diabetes, and certain types of cancer. Fiber also keeps us feeling fuller for longer, making it an essential element for those looking to manage their weight and control their appetite.

What You'll Find Inside

Within the pages of "High-Fiber Wholesome Recipes," you'll discover an array of recipes carefully crafted to provide you with the fiber your body craves.
Start your day with hearty fiber-packed colorful salads and nutrient-rich soups, enjoy satisfying main courses that showcase the variety and versatility of high-fiber ingredients.. Whether you're a seasoned cook or a novice in the kitchen, the recipes in this cookbook are easy to follow, ensuring that your journey toward a healthier lifestyle is both enjoyable and attainable.

What Sets This Cookbook Apart

What sets "High-Fiber Wholesome Recipes" apart from other cookbooks is the focus on both nutrition and flavor. Each recipe has been thoughtfully curated to include ingredients that are not only high in fiber but also bursting with taste. We believe that a healthy diet should never compromise on enjoyment.

Contents

Introduction 4
Sweetcorn Fritters With Eggs & Black Bean Salsa 10
Sautéed Broccoli With Peanut Sauce 11
Chickpea And Spinach Curry 12
Vegetarian Chili 13
Quinoa And Black Bean Salad 14
Sweet Potato And Black Bean Tacos 15
Kale And White Bean Soup 16
Roasted Root Vegetable Panzanella 17
Stuffed Bell Peppers With Brown Rice And Lentils 18
Roasted Vegetable Quinoa Bowl 19
Butternut Squash And Black Bean Enchiladas 20
Pea & Spinach Carbonara 21
Quinoa Chickpea Salad With Roasted Red Pepper Hummus Dressing 22
Spinach-Strawberry Salad With Feta & Walnuts 23
Prosciutto Pizza With Corn & Arugula 24
Tex-Mex Pasta Salad 25
Cherry Tomato & Garlic Pasta 26
Whole-Wheat Pasta With Lentil Bolognese 27
Kale, Quinoa & Apple Salad 28
Superfood Chopped Salad With Salmon & Creamy Garlic Dressing 29
Greek Salad With Edamame 30
Goddess Veggie Bowls With Chicken 31
Black Bean And Corn Salad 32
 Quinoa And Black Bean Stuffed Peppers 33
Bean Burritos 34

Minestrone With Turkey 35
Spinach And Mushroom Quesadillas 36
Creamy Lentil Curry With Roasted Butternut Squash 37
Roasted Beet And Chickpea Salad 38
Eggplant And Zucchini Ratatouille 39
Sweet Potato And Black Bean Tacos 40
Broccoli And Cheddar Stuffed Baked Potatoes 41
Vegan Lentil And Vegetable Stir-Fry 42
Spicy Chorizo-And-Pinto Bean Chili 43
Slow-Cooker Black Bean And Spinach Enchiladas 44
Glazed Brussels Sprouts On Olive Oil-Fried Bread 45
Cauliflower And Chickpea Stew With Couscous 46
Kale Salad With Roasted Sweet Potato & Black Beans 47
Spring Vegetable Minestra With Mint & Basil Pistou 48
Cheesy Marinara Beans 49
Jackfruit Barbacoa Burrito Bowls 50
White Bean & Sun-Dried Tomato Gnocchi 51
Creamy Spinach Pasta With White Beans 52
Quinoa, Avocado & Chickpea Salad Over Mixed Greens 53
Vegan Chickpea Stew 54
Whole Wheat Pasta With Tomato Sauce And Vegetables 55
Lentil & Sweet Potato Shepherd's Pie 56
Grilled Eggplant Salad With Halloumi & Tomatoes 57
Feta And Watermelon Grain Bowls 58
Roasted Root Veggie Quinoa Bowls 59
Rice Bowl With Chipotle Black Beans 60
Green Salad 61
Roasted Vegetable Bowls With Pesto 62
Black Bean & Slaw Bagel 63

Chopped Salad With Sriracha Tofu & Peanut Dressing ... 64
Chipotle Tofu Chilaquiles ... 65
Roasted Sweet Potato & Kale Hash ... 66
Cheesy Broccoli Hashbrown Bake ... 67
Curried Quinoa Chickpea Burgers ... 68
Grilled Romaine Caesar Salad With Herbed White Beans ... 69
Roasted Plantain & Black Bean Vegan Bowl ... 70
Veggie Niçoise Salad With Red Curry Green Beans ... 71
Chickpea And Vegetable Coconut Curry ... 72
Salmon Bowl With Farro, Black Beans And Tahini Dressing ... 73
Harissa Chickpea Stew With Eggplant And Millet ... 74
Lemon-Tahini Salad With Lentils, Beets And Carrots ... 75
Chicken Avocado Black Bean Salad ... 76
Quinoa Bowl With Avocado Sauce ... 77
Cauliflower Chicken Nachos ... 78
Lemon-Roasted Vegetable Hummus Bowls ... 79
Broccoli With Balsamic Mushrooms ... 80
Roasted Butternut Squash Salad With Burrata ... 81
Kale & Shaved Brussels Sprouts Salad With Avocado Caesar Dressing ... 82
Feta & Olive Stuffed Eggplant ... 83
Frittata With Asparagus, Leek & Ricotta ... 84
Cheesy Marinara Beans ... 85
Broccoli & Quinoa Casserole ... 86
Piled-High Vegetable Pitas ... 87
Summer Vegetable Gnocchi Salad ... 88
Eggplant Curry ... 89
Grilled Cauliflower Steaks With Almond Pesto & Butter Beans ... 90
Black Bean Bulgur Salad ... 91
Crab Louie Salad ... 92
Succotash Salad With Grilled Sirloin ... 93
White Bean & Veggie Salad ... 94
Egg, Spinach & Cheddar Sandwich ... 95

Buttery Shrimp With Marinated White Beans 96
Pot Chicken Sausage And Beans 97
Creamy Swiss Chard Gratin With Crispy Gnocchi 98
Charred Cauliflower Tacos With Romesco Salsa 99
Farro Salad With Roasted Root Vegetables 100
Eggplant And Lentil Stew With Pomegranate Molasses 101
Tagliatelle With Tomatoes And Greens 102
Refried Bean Tostadas 103
Two-Bean Tomato Bake 104
Red Potatoes With Beans 105
Black Bean Pasta 106
Farro Kale Salad 107
Smoky Beans & Baked Eggs 108
Griddled Cornbread With Devilled Eggs & Avocado 109
Conclusion **110**

SWEETCORN FRITTERS WITH EGGS & BLACK BEAN SALSA

PREP TIME: 10 MINS   **COOK TIME:** 20 MINS   **SERVINGS:** 4

Treat your taste buds to a delightful combination of flavors and a healthy dose of fiber with these Sweetcorn Fritters served alongside a zesty Black Bean Salsa. This dish not only satisfies your palate but also provides a nutritious kick with its rich fiber content. Enjoy the crispiness of sweetcorn fritters paired with the freshness of a homemade black bean salsa for a wholesome and satisfying meal.

INGREDIENTS

For the fritters & eggs
- 1 tsp rapeseed oil
- 1 small red onion (85g), finely chopped
- 1 red pepper, deseeded and finely diced
- 100g wholemeal self-raising flour
- 1 tsp smoked paprika
- 1 tsp ground coriander
- 1 tsp baking powder
- 325g can sweetcorn, drained
- 6 large eggs

For the salsa
- 1 small red onion (85g), finely chopped
- 4 tomatoes (320g), chopped
- 2 x 400g cans black beans, drained
- 1 lime, zested and juiced
- ½ x 30g pack coriander, chopped

Nutritional Value: 322 calories | 27g protein. | 15g fat | 35g carbohydrate | Fiber: 25g

INGREDIENTS

1. Heat the oven to 200C/180C fan/gas 6 and line a large baking tray with baking parchment.
2. Heat the oil in a small pan and fry the onion and pepper for 5 mins until softened. Meanwhile, mix the flour, spices and baking powder in a bowl. Add the onions, pepper, corn and 2 of the eggs, then mix together well.
3. Spoon eight mounds of the mixture onto the baking tray, well spaced apart, then flatten slightly with the back of the spoon. Bake for 20 mins until set and golden.
4. Meanwhile, mix together the salsa ingredients and poach 2 of the remaining eggs to your liking. If you're following a healthy diet plan, serve four fritters on the day you make them, topped with half the salsa and the poached eggs.
5. Chill the remaining fritters for another day. Reheat them in a pan or microwave and serve with 2 more poached eggs and the remaining salsa.

SAUTÉED BROCCOLI WITH PEANUT SAUCE

PREP TIME: 15 MINS   **COOK TIME:** 30 MINS   **SERVINGS:** 2

Enjoy the delightful flavors of sautéed broccoli combined with a rich and creamy peanut sauce. This high-fiber dish is not only delicious but also incredibly nutritious, making it a perfect addition to your high-fiber recipe collection.

INGREDIENTS

- 8 cups broccoli florets (2-inch pieces)
- 2 tablespoons toasted sesame oil
- 1 cup sliced red bell pepper
- ½ cup sliced yellow onion
- 3 medium cloves garlic, chopped
- 3 tablespoons smooth natural peanut butter
- 2 ½ tablespoons reduced-sodium tamari
- 2 tablespoons rice vinegar
- 1 tablespoon light brown sugar
- 1 teaspoon cornstarch
- 1 tablespoon toasted sesame seeds

INGREDIENTS

1. Bring 1 inch of water to a boil in a large pot fitted with a steamer basket. Add broccoli, cover and cook until tender-crisp, 3 to 4 minutes.
2. Meanwhile, heat oil in a large skillet over medium-high heat. Add bell pepper, onion and garlic; cook, stirring often, until the vegetables begin to soften, about 3 minutes.
3. Add the steamed broccoli and cook, stirring, for 3 minutes. Whisk peanut butter, tamari, vinegar, sugar and cornstarch in a small bowl until smooth. Stir into the vegetables.
4. Cook, stirring, until the sauce thickens, about 1 minute. Sprinkle with sesame seeds.

Nutritional Value: 300 calories | 25g protein. | 8g fat | 28g carbohydrate | Fiber: 25g

CHICKPEA AND SPINACH CURRY

PREP TIME: 15 MINS **COOK TIME:** 25 MINS **SERVINGS:** 4

This Chickpea and Spinach Curry is a delicious and nutritious high-fiber dish that's perfect for a healthy meal. Packed with chickpeas and spinach, it's a flavorful option that's easy to prepare.

INGREDIENTS

- 2 cans (15 ounces each) of chickpeas, drained and rinsed
- 1 onion, finely chopped
- 3 cloves garlic, minced
- 1-inch piece of fresh ginger, grated
- 1 can (14 ounces) of diced tomatoes
- 1 can (14 ounces) of coconut milk
- 2 cups fresh spinach leaves
- 2 tablespoons vegetable oil
- 2 teaspoons curry powder
- 1 teaspoon ground cumin
- 1 teaspoon ground coriander
- 1/2 teaspoon turmeric
- Salt and pepper to taste
- Fresh cilantro leaves for garnish
- Cooked rice or naan bread for serving (optional)

INGREDIENTS

1. In a large skillet or pan, heat the vegetable oil over medium heat. Add the chopped onion and cook for about 3-4 minutes until it becomes translucent. Stir in the minced garlic and grated ginger. Cook for an additional 1-2 minutes until fragrant.
2. Add the curry powder, ground cumin, ground coriander, and turmeric. Stir well and cook for another 1-2 minutes to toast the spices.
3. Pour in the diced tomatoes and coconut milk. Stir to combine all the ingredients and bring the mixture to a simmer.
4. Add the drained chickpeas to the pan. Allow the curry to simmer for about 15-20 minutes, stirring occasionally, until it thickens and the chickpeas are heated through.
5. Fold in the fresh spinach leaves and cook for an additional 2-3 minutes until the spinach wilts.
6. Season with salt and pepper to taste. Adjust the seasoning to your preference.
7. Serve hot, garnished with fresh cilantro leaves. You can enjoy this Chickpea and Spinach Curry on its own or with cooked rice or naan bread.

Nutritional Value: 360 calories | 25g protein. | 15g fat | 33g carbohydrate | Fiber: 26g

VEGETARIAN CHILI

PREP TIME: 15 MINS   **COOK TIME:** 35 MINS   **SERVINGS:** 4

Vegetarian Chili is a hearty and nutritious dish that's perfect for those seeking a high-fiber meal packed with flavor and wholesome ingredients. This recipe combines a colorful medley of vegetables, beans, and spices to create a satisfying chili that's not only delicious but also incredibly fiber-rich, with over 30 grams of fiber per serving. Whether you're a dedicated vegetarian or simply looking to incorporate more fiber into your diet, this chili is a tasty and filling choice that won't disappoint.

INGREDIENTS

- 2 tablespoons olive oil
- 1 medium onion, chopped
- 3 cloves garlic, minced
- 1 red bell pepper, chopped
- 1 yellow bell pepper, chopped
- 1 green bell pepper, chopped
- 1 jalapeño pepper, finely chopped (optional, for heat)
- 2 carrots, diced
- 2 celery stalks, diced
- 1 zucchini, diced
- 1 cup frozen corn kernels
- 2 (15-ounce) cans black beans, drained and rinsed
- 2 (15-ounce) cans kidney beans, drained and rinsed
- 1 (28-ounce) can crushed tomatoes
- 1 (14-ounce) can diced tomatoes
- 2 cups vegetable broth
- 2 tablespoons chili powder
- 1 tablespoon cumin
- 1 teaspoon paprika
- 1 teaspoon oregano
- Salt and pepper to taste
- Chopped fresh cilantro, for garnish
- Shredded cheddar cheese (optional, for serving)
- Sour cream (optional, for serving)
- Sliced green onions (optional, for serving)
- Avocado slices (optional, for serving)

INGREDIENTS

1. Heat the olive oil in a large pot or Dutch oven over medium heat. Add the chopped onion and garlic and sauté for 2-3 minutes, until fragrant.
2. Add the chopped red, yellow, and green bell peppers, as well as the jalapeño pepper if using. Sauté for another 3-4 minutes until the peppers begin to soften.
3. Stir in the diced carrots, celery, zucchini, and frozen corn. Cook for an additional 5 minutes, allowing the vegetables to start to soften.
4. Add the drained and rinsed black beans and kidney beans to the pot, along with the crushed tomatoes, diced tomatoes, and vegetable broth. Stir to combine.
5. Season the chili with chili powder, cumin, paprika, oregano, salt, and pepper. Adjust the seasoning to taste. If you like it spicier, you can add more chili powder or jalapeño at this stage.
6. Bring the chili to a boil, then reduce the heat to low. Cover and simmer for 20-25 minutes, stirring occasionally, until the vegetables are tender and the flavors meld together.
7. Serve the high-fiber vegetarian chili hot, garnished with chopped fresh cilantro. Optionally, top each bowl with shredded cheddar cheese, a dollop of sour cream, sliced green onions, and avocado slices for added flavor.

Nutritional Value: 355 calories | 27g protein. | 12g fat | 25g carbohydrate | Fiber: 27g

QUINOA AND BLACK BEAN SALAD

PREP TIME: 15 MINS   **COOK TIME:** 30 MINS   **SERVINGS:** 4

This Quinoa and Black Bean Salad is not only delicious but also packed with fiber, thanks to the combination of quinoa, black beans, and a medley of vegetables. It's a perfect dish for those looking to increase their fiber intake while enjoying a tasty, nutritious meal.

INGREDIENTS

- 1 cup quinoa, rinsed and drained
- 2 cups water
- 1 can (15 ounces) black beans, drained and rinsed
- 1 red bell pepper, diced
- 1 yellow bell pepper, diced
- 1 cup cherry tomatoes, halved
- 1 cup cucumber, diced
- 1/2 cup red onion, finely chopped
- 1/4 cup fresh cilantro, chopped
- 1/4 cup fresh parsley, chopped
- 1/4 cup extra-virgin olive oil
- 3 tablespoons fresh lime juice
- 2 cloves garlic, minced
- 1 teaspoon ground cumin
- Salt and pepper to taste

INGREDIENTS

1. In a medium saucepan, combine the rinsed quinoa and 2 cups of water. Bring it to a boil, then reduce the heat to low, cover, and simmer for about 12-15 minutes, or until the quinoa is tender and the water is absorbed. Remove from heat and let it cool.
2. In a large mixing bowl, combine the cooked quinoa, black beans, diced red and yellow bell peppers, cherry tomatoes, cucumber, red onion, cilantro, and parsley.
3. In a separate small bowl, whisk together the extra-virgin olive oil, fresh lime juice, minced garlic, ground cumin, salt, and pepper.
4. Pour the dressing over the quinoa and vegetable mixture. Gently toss to combine, ensuring all the ingredients are coated evenly.
5. Taste and adjust the seasoning with more salt and pepper if needed.
6. Serve the Quinoa and Black Bean Salad chilled or at room temperature. It can be enjoyed as a light meal on its own or as a side dish alongside grilled chicken or fish.

Nutritional Value: 315 calories | 21g protein. | 13g fat | 45g carbohydrate | Fiber: 28g

SWEET POTATO AND BLACK BEAN TACOS

PREP TIME: 15 MINS   **COOK TIME:** 30 MINS   **SERVINGS:** 4

These Sweet Potato and Black Bean Tacos are a delicious and nutritious way to enjoy a high-fiber meal. Packed with flavor and loaded with fiber from sweet potatoes and black beans, these tacos are sure to satisfy your taste buds and keep you feeling full and energized.

INGREDIENTS

- For the Filling:
- 2 medium sweet potatoes, peeled and diced
- 1 can (15 ounces) black beans, drained and rinsed
- 1 tablespoon olive oil
- 1 small onion, diced
- 2 cloves garlic, minced
- 1 teaspoon ground cumin
- 1/2 teaspoon chili powder
- Salt and pepper to taste
  For the Tacos:
- 8 small whole wheat or corn tortillas
- 1 cup shredded lettuce
- 1 cup diced tomatoes
- 1/2 cup diced red onion
- 1/2 cup chopped fresh cilantro
- 1 cup plain Greek yogurt or sour cream (optional)
- Lime wedges for garnish (optional)

Nutritional Value: 350 calories | 25g protein. | 15g fat | 33g carbohydrate | Fiber: 25g

INGREDIENTS

1. In a large skillet, heat the olive oil over medium heat. Add the diced onion and cook for 2-3 minutes until it becomes translucent.
2. Add the minced garlic, diced sweet potatoes, ground cumin, chili powder, salt, and pepper to the skillet. Cook, stirring occasionally, for about 15-20 minutes or until the sweet potatoes are tender and slightly crispy on the outside.
3. Once the sweet potatoes are cooked, add the black beans to the skillet and stir to combine. Cook for an additional 2-3 minutes until the beans are heated through.
4. Warm the tortillas in a dry skillet or microwave according to the package instructions.
5. To assemble the tacos, spoon the sweet potato and black bean mixture onto each tortilla. Top with shredded lettuce, diced tomatoes, diced red onion, and chopped cilantro.
6. If desired, add a dollop of plain Greek yogurt or sour cream on top of each taco for a creamy finish.
7. Serve the Sweet Potato and Black Bean Tacos with lime wedges on the side for a burst of citrus flavor.

KALE AND WHITE BEAN SOUP

PREP TIME: 15 MINS   **COOK TIME:** 30 MINS   **SERVINGS:** 4

This hearty Kale and White Bean Soup is not only delicious but also packed with fiber from plenty of beans and vegetables. It's a perfect choice for a healthy and satisfying meal.

INGREDIENTS

- 1 tablespoon olive oil
- 1 onion, chopped
- 2 cloves garlic, minced
- 3 cups vegetable broth
- 2 cups water
- 2 cups kale, chopped
- 2 cans (15 ounces each) white beans, drained and rinsed
- 1 can (14.5 ounces) diced tomatoes
- 1 teaspoon dried thyme
- 1 teaspoon dried rosemary
- Salt and pepper to taste

INGREDIENTS

1. In a large soup pot, heat the olive oil over medium heat. Add the chopped onion and garlic, and sauté until they become translucent, about 3-4 minutes.
2. Pour in the vegetable broth and water, and bring the mixture to a boil. Add the chopped kale, white beans, diced tomatoes, dried thyme, and dried rosemary.
3. Reduce the heat to a simmer and let the soup cook for 20-25 minutes, allowing the flavors to meld together.
4. Season the soup with salt and pepper to taste. Adjust the seasoning as needed.
5. Serve the Kale and White Bean Soup hot. You can garnish it with a drizzle of olive oil, grated Parmesan cheese, or a sprinkle of red pepper flakes if desired.

Nutritional Value: 260 calories | 21g protein. | 15g fat | 43g carbohydrate | Fiber: 25g

ROASTED ROOT VEGETABLE PANZANELLA

PREP TIME: 10 MINS

COOK TIME: 30 MINS

SERVINGS: 4

Enjoy the vibrant flavors of roasted root vegetables and crispy croutons, paired with a delightful tahini dressing, in this hearty Roasted Root Vegetable Panzanella.

INGREDIENTS

Veggies:
- 3 cups peeled and chopped root vegetables (e.g., beets, carrots, sweet potatoes)
- 1 medium leek, halved, rinsed, and chopped into 1/4-inch slices
- 1 tablespoon avocado or olive oil
- A pinch of salt and black pepper
- 2 sprigs fresh rosemary, chopped

Chickpeas:
- 1 (15-ounce) can chickpeas, rinsed, drained, and patted dry with a towel
- 1 tablespoon avocado or olive oil
- A pinch of salt and black pepper
- 1 sprig fresh rosemary, chopped (or substitute dried)
- 5 cloves garlic, crushed or roughly chopped (optional)
- Croutons: 2 cups day-old sturdy bread, cubed
- 1 teaspoon avocado oil
- A pinch of salt and pepper

Dressing:
- 1/4 cup tahini (cashew butter)
- 1 ½ teaspoons whole grain mustard
- 2-3 tablespoons lemon juice
- 1 teaspoon apple cider vinegar
- 2-3 teaspoons maple syrup
- A pinch of salt and pepper
- 2-4 tablespoons water to thin

Greens:
- 1 large bundle of kale, torn into bite-size pieces, with large stems removed (1 large bundle is about 8 cups or 200g)
- 2 tablespoons lemon juice (optional)

DIRECTIONS

1. Preheat your oven to 400 degrees F (204 C) and position one rack near the top of the oven and another in the top/center. Line two large baking sheets with parchment paper.
2. Chop the root vegetables and thinly slice the leek, making sure to rinse away any residual dirt. Add them to one of the prepared baking sheets. Sprinkle with oil, salt, pepper, and rosemary. Toss to coat.
3. Spread the vegetables in an even layer on the bottom rack of the oven. Bake for 20-25 minutes or until they are tender, slightly caramelized, and golden brown. Flip/toss near the 15-minute mark for even cooking.
4. In a medium mixing bowl, add the rinsed, dried chickpeas and top with oil, salt, pepper, rosemary, and crushed garlic (optional). Toss to combine, then add them to one half of the other prepared baking sheet. Place in the top/center rack of the oven and bake for about 20 minutes or until golden brown.
5. While the veggies and chickpeas are roasting, prepare the dressing. Combine tahini, grainy mustard, lemon juice (starting with the lesser amount), apple cider vinegar, maple syrup (starting with the lesser amount), salt, and pepper in a bowl.
6. Whisk to combine, adding water until the dressing is pourable. Adjust seasonings to taste.
7. In the same mixing bowl used for the chickpeas, add the cubed bread and toss with a little oil, salt, and pepper. Add them to the other half of the baking sheet with the chickpeas and bake for 8-10 minutes or until toasty and golden brown.
8. If using kale or other greens, add them to a large mixing bowl. Optionally, dress with a bit of lemon juice, salt, and pepper. Massage for 1-2 minutes for a more tender texture and improved digestibility.
9. Top the greens with the roasted vegetables, chickpeas, and croutons. Add half of the dressing, toss, and reserve the other half for serving.
10. This dish is best enjoyed fresh, but if saving for later, store all components separately to prevent sogginess. The dressing will keep for 5-7 days, croutons for up to 2 days when loosely covered at room temperature, and the salad for 2-3 days. This dish is not freezer-friendly.

Nutritional Value: 370 calories | 21g protein. | 25g fat | 44g carbohydrate | Fiber: 28g

STUFFED BELL PEPPERS WITH BROWN RICE AND LENTILS

PREP TIME: 20 MINS   **COOK TIME:** 40 MINS   **SERVINGS:** 4

These Stuffed Bell Peppers with Brown Rice and Lentils are a nutritious and delicious way to incorporate high-fiber ingredients into your meal. Packed with the goodness of beans and vegetables, this recipe is not only satisfying but also incredibly healthy.

INGREDIENTS

- 4 large bell peppers (any color)
- 1 cup brown rice
- 1/2 cup brown lentils
- 1 onion, finely chopped
- 2 cloves garlic, minced
- 1 cup canned black beans, drained and rinsed
- 1 cup diced tomatoes (canned or fresh)
- 1/2 cup corn kernels (fresh or frozen)
- 1 teaspoon cumin powder
- 1 teaspoon chili powder (adjust to taste)
- Salt and pepper to taste
- 1 cup vegetable broth
- 1 cup shredded cheese (optional, for topping)
- Fresh cilantro or parsley for garnish (optional)

Nutritional Value: 350 calories | 25g protein. | 15g fat | 30g carbohydrate | Fiber: 25g

INGREDIENTS

1. Start by preheating your oven to 375°F (190°C). Wash the bell peppers and cut off the tops. Remove the seeds and membranes from the inside. Set aside.
2. In a medium saucepan, combine the brown rice and lentils with 2 1/2 cups of water. Bring to a boil, then reduce the heat to low, cover, and simmer for about 20-25 minutes or until both rice and lentils are tender and the water is absorbed.
3. While the rice and lentils are cooking, heat a large skillet over medium heat. Add a drizzle of olive oil if desired. Add the chopped onion and garlic and sauté until they become translucent, about 3-4 minutes.
4. Stir in the cumin powder, chili powder, salt, and pepper. Cook for another 2 minutes until the spices become fragrant.
5. Add the diced tomatoes, black beans, and corn kernels to the skillet. Cook for an additional 5 minutes, allowing the flavors to meld together.
6. Once the rice and lentil mixture is ready, add it to the skillet with the vegetable mixture. Stir well to combine. If the mixture seems dry, add a splash of vegetable broth to moisten it.
7. Carefully stuff each bell pepper with the rice and lentil mixture, packing it down gently. Place the stuffed peppers in a baking dish.
8. Pour the remaining vegetable broth into the bottom of the baking dish to create a steamy environment for the peppers.
9. Cover the baking dish with aluminum foil and bake in the preheated oven for 25-30 minutes or until the peppers are tender.
10. If using cheese, remove the foil, sprinkle the shredded cheese on top of each stuffed pepper, and return them to the oven. Bake for an additional 5-7 minutes, or until the cheese is melted and bubbly.
11. Remove the stuffed bell peppers from the oven, garnish with fresh cilantro or parsley if desired, and serve hot.

ROASTED VEGETABLE QUINOA BOWL

PREP TIME: 15 MINS **COOK TIME:** 25 MINS **SERVINGS:** 4

This Roasted Vegetable Quinoa Bowl is a wholesome and flavorful dish packed with fiber, featuring a medley of roasted vegetables, fluffy quinoa, and a tasty dressing. It's a perfect choice for a healthy and satisfying meal that's as delicious as it is nutritious.

INGREDIENTS

- For the Roasted Vegetables:
- 2 cups mixed vegetables (e.g., bell peppers, zucchini, broccoli, carrots), chopped into bite-sized pieces
- 2 tablespoons olive oil
- 1 teaspoon dried thyme
- Salt and pepper to taste
  For the Quinoa:
- 1 cup quinoa, rinsed
- 2 cups water
- 1/2 teaspoon salt
  For the Dressing:
- 2 tablespoons olive oil
- 1 tablespoon balsamic vinegar
- 1 clove garlic, minced
- 1 teaspoon honey
- Salt and pepper to taste
  For Assembly:
- 1 can (15 oz) black beans, drained and rinsed
- 1 cup cherry tomatoes, halved
- 1/4 cup fresh basil leaves, chopped
- 1/4 cup feta cheese (optional)

Nutritional Value: 320 calories | 25g protein. | 15g fat | 33g carbohydrate | Fiber: 26g

INGREDIENTS

1. Preheat the Oven: Preheat your oven to 425°F (220°C). Roast the Vegetables: In a large bowl, toss the mixed vegetables with olive oil, dried thyme, salt, and pepper.
2. Spread them evenly on a baking sheet and roast in the preheated oven for about 20-25 minutes or until they are tender and slightly caramelized.
3. Cook the Quinoa: While the vegetables are roasting, rinse the quinoa under cold water. In a medium saucepan, combine the rinsed quinoa, water, and salt.
4. Bring to a boil, then reduce heat, cover, and simmer for 15 minutes or until the quinoa is cooked and the liquid is absorbed. Remove from heat and let it sit, covered, for 5 minutes. Fluff with a fork.
5. Prepare the Dressing: In a small bowl, whisk together olive oil, balsamic vinegar, minced garlic, honey, salt, and pepper. Set aside.
6. Assemble the Bowl: In each serving bowl, start with a portion of cooked quinoa.
7. Top with roasted vegetables, black beans, cherry tomatoes, and fresh basil. Drizzle with Dressing: Drizzle the dressing over the bowl and sprinkle with feta cheese if desired.
8. Serve: Serve the Roasted Vegetable Quinoa Bowl immediately, and enjoy your fiber-rich, nutritious meal!

BUTTERNUT SQUASH AND BLACK BEAN ENCHILADAS

PREP TIME: 20 MINS   **COOK TIME:** 30 MINS   **SERVINGS:** 4

These Butternut Squash and Black Bean Enchiladas are a delicious and nutritious way to incorporate more fiber into your diet. Packed with wholesome ingredients like butternut squash, black beans, and vegetables, this dish is not only high in fiber but also bursting with flavor.

INGREDIENTS

- For the Filling:
- 2 cups diced butternut squash
- 1 can (15 ounces) black beans, drained and rinsed
- 1 cup diced red bell pepper
- 1 cup diced onion
- 2 cloves garlic, minced
- 1 teaspoon ground cumin
- 1/2 teaspoon chili powder
- Salt and pepper to taste
- 1 tablespoon olive oil
- For the Enchilada Sauce:
- 1 can (15 ounces) tomato sauce
- 1/2 cup vegetable broth
- 1 teaspoon ground cumin
- 1/2 teaspoon chili powder
- Salt and pepper to taste
- For Assembly:
- 8 whole wheat or corn tortillas
- 1 1/2 cups shredded cheddar cheese (optional)
- Fresh cilantro leaves for garnish (optional)

Nutritional Value: 312 calories | 26g protein. | 23g fat | 30g carbohydrate | Fiber: 26g

INGREDIENTS

1. Preheat your oven to 375°F (190°C). In a large skillet, heat the olive oil over medium heat. Add the diced onion, bell pepper, and minced garlic. Sauté for about 2-3 minutes until they start to soften.
2. Add the diced butternut squash to the skillet and continue cooking for another 5-7 minutes until the squash becomes tender and slightly caramelized.
3. Stir in the black beans, ground cumin, chili powder, salt, and pepper. Cook for an additional 2-3 minutes, allowing the flavors to meld together. Remove from heat.
4. In a separate saucepan, combine the tomato sauce, vegetable broth, ground cumin, chili powder, salt, and pepper. Heat over low-medium heat, stirring occasionally, until the sauce is warmed through.
5. To assemble the enchiladas, spoon a generous portion of the butternut squash and black bean filling onto each tortilla, then roll it up tightly. Place the filled tortillas seam-side down in a baking dish.
6. Pour the enchilada sauce evenly over the rolled tortillas. If desired, sprinkle shredded cheddar cheese on top.
7. Cover the baking dish with aluminum foil and bake in the preheated oven for 20-25 minutes, or until the enchiladas are heated through and the cheese is melted.
8. Garnish with fresh cilantro leaves, if you like. Serve hot, and enjoy your high-fiber Butternut Squash and Black Bean Enchiladas!

PEA & SPINACH CARBONARA

PREP TIME: 20 MINS   **COOK TIME:** 40 MINS   **SERVINGS:** 4

This Pea & Spinach Carbonara is a delightful twist on the classic carbonara pasta dish. Packed with high-fiber ingredients like peas and spinach, it's a healthy and delicious option for those looking to boost their fiber intake.

INGREDIENTS

- 1 ½ tablespoons extra-virgin olive oil
- ½ cup panko breadcrumbs, preferably whole-wheat
- 1 small clove garlic, minced
- 8 tablespoons grated Parmesan cheese, divided
- 3 tablespoons finely chopped fresh parsley
- 3 large egg yolks
- 1 large egg
- ½ teaspoon ground pepper
- ¼ teaspoon salt
- 1 (9 ounce) package fresh tagliatelle or linguine
- 8 cups baby spinach
- 1 cup peas (fresh or frozen)

INGREDIENTS

1. Put 10 cups of water in a large pot and bring to a boil over high heat. Meanwhile, heat oil in a large skillet over medium-high heat.
2. Add breadcrumbs and garlic; cook, stirring frequently, until toasted, about 2 minutes. Transfer to a small bowl and stir in 2 tablespoons Parmesan and parsley. Set aside.
3. Whisk the remaining 6 tablespoons Parmesan, egg yolks, egg, pepper and salt in a medium bowl.
4. Cook pasta in the boiling water, stirring occasionally, for 1 minute. Add spinach and peas and cook until the pasta is tender, about 1 minute more.
5. Reserve 1/4 cup of the cooking water. Drain and place in a large bowl. Slowly whisk the reserved cooking water into the egg mixture.
6. Gradually add the mixture to the pasta, tossing with tongs to combine. Serve topped with the reserved breadcrumb mixture.

Nutritional Value: 320 calories | 25g protein. | 15g fat | 33g carbohydrate | Fiber: 26g

QUINOA CHICKPEA SALAD WITH ROASTED RED PEPPER HUMMUS DRESSING

PREP TIME: 10 MINS **COOK TIME:** 10 MINS **SERVINGS:** 2

This Quinoa Chickpea Salad with Roasted Red Pepper Hummus Dressing is a delightful, high-fiber dish that combines the nutty flavor of quinoa, the protein-packed goodness of chickpeas, and the zesty kick of roasted red pepper hummus. It's a perfect choice for a healthy and satisfying meal.

INGREDIENTS

- 2 tablespoons hummus, original or roasted red pepper flavor
- 1 tablespoon lemon juice
- 1 tablespoon chopped roasted red pepper
- 2 cups mixed salad greens
- ½ cup cooked quinoa
- ½ cup chickpeas, rinsed
- 1 tablespoon unsalted sunflower seeds
- 1 tablespoon chopped fresh parsley
- Pinch of salt
- Pinch of ground pepper

INGREDIENTS

1. Stir hummus, lemon juice and red peppers in a small dish. Thin with water to desired consistency for dressing.
2. Arrange greens, quinoa and chickpeas in a large bowl. Top with sunflower seeds, parsley, salt and pepper. Serve with the dressing.

Nutritional Value: 361 calories | 21g protein. | 16g fat | 54g carbohydrate | Fiber: 27g

SPINACH-STRAWBERRY SALAD WITH FETA & WALNUTS

PREP TIME: 15 MINS **COOK TIME:** 30 MINS **SERVINGS:** 2

This Spinach-Strawberry Salad with Feta & Walnuts is a delightful high-fiber dish that combines the freshness of spinach and strawberries with the creamy richness of feta cheese and the crunch of walnuts. It's a perfect choice for a healthy and satisfying meal.

INGREDIENTS

- 1 ½ tablespoons extra-virgin olive oil
- 1 tablespoon best-quality balsamic vinegar
- 2 teaspoons finely chopped shallot
- ¼ teaspoon salt
- ¼ teaspoon ground pepper
- 6 cups baby spinach
- 1 cup sliced strawberries
- ¼ cup crumbled feta cheese
- ¼ cup toasted chopped walnuts

INGREDIENTS

1. Whisk oil, vinegar, shallot, salt and pepper in a large bowl. Let stand for 5 to 10 minutes to allow shallots to soften and mellow a bit.
2. Add spinach, strawberries, feta and walnuts to the bowl and toss to coat with the dressing.

Nutritional Value: 200 calories | 21g protein. | 12g fat | 21g carbohydrate | Fiber: 25g

PROSCIUTTO PIZZA WITH CORN & ARUGULA

PREP TIME: 20 MINS **COOK TIME:** 40 MINS **SERVINGS:** 4

This Prosciutto Pizza with Corn & Arugula is a delightful combination of savory prosciutto, sweet corn, and peppery arugula. With a high-fiber crust and plenty of fresh vegetables, it's a healthy and satisfying choice for pizza lovers.

INGREDIENTS

- 1 pound pizza dough, preferably whole-wheat
- 2 tablespoons extra-virgin olive oil, divided
- 1 clove garlic, minced
- 1 cup part-skim shredded mozzarella cheese
- 1 cup fresh corn kernels
- 1 ounce very thinly sliced prosciutto, torn into 1-inch pieces
- 1 ½ cups arugula
- ½ cup torn fresh basil
- ¼ teaspoon ground pepper

INGREDIENTS

1. Preheat grill to medium-high. (Or to bake instead, see Tips.) Roll dough out on a lightly floured surface into a 12-inch oval. Transfer to a lightly floured large baking sheet.
2. Combine 1 tablespoon oil and garlic in a small bowl. Bring the dough, the garlic oil, cheese, corn and prosciutto to the grill. Oil the grill rack (see Tips). Transfer the crust to the grill.
3. Grill the dough until puffed and lightly browned, 1 to 2 minutes. Flip the crust over and spread the garlic oil on it. Top with the cheese, corn and prosciutto.
4. Grill, covered, until the cheese is melted and the crust is lightly browned on the bottom, 2 to 3 minutes more. Return the pizza to the baking sheet.
5. Top the pizza with arugula, basil and pepper. Drizzle with the remaining 1 tablespoon oil.

Nutritional Value: 360 calories | 25g protein. | 20g fat | 53g carbohydrate | Fiber: 27g

TEX-MEX PASTA SALAD

PREP TIME: 10 MINS   **COOK TIME:** 15 MINS   **SERVINGS:** 4

Tex-Mex Pasta Salad is a delightful and nutritious dish that combines the flavors of Texan and Mexican cuisine with the goodness of high-fiber ingredients. Packed with beans and vegetables, this recipe is a wholesome option for a light lunch or a flavorful side dish for any occasion.

INGREDIENTS

- 1 tablespoon tomatillo salsa
- 1 tablespoon low-fat plain Greek yogurt
- 1 cup cherry tomatoes, halved
- ¾ cup chopped red bell pepper
- ¾ cup frozen shelled edamame (4 oz.), cooked according to package directions, drained and cooled
- ½ cup cooked orzo, preferably whole-wheat, cooled
- ¼ cup chopped red onion
- 2 tablespoons shredded pepper Jack cheese
- ⅛ teaspoon salt
- ⅛ teaspoon ground pepper
- Hot sauce, to taste
- 1 tablespoon toasted pepitas (see Tip)
- Lime wedge, for serving

Nutritional Value: 350 calories | 25g protein. | 15g fat | 43g carbohydrate | Fiber: 26g

INGREDIENTS

1. Whisk salsa and yogurt in a small bowl. Set aside. Combine tomatoes, bell pepper, edamame, orzo, onion, and cheese in a bowl.
2. Add salt, pepper, and the salsa dressing; toss to combine. Season with hot sauce to taste, sprinkle with pepitas, and serve with lime wedge, if desired.

CHERRY TOMATO & GARLIC PASTA

PREP TIME: 20 MINS   **COOK TIME:** 40 MINS   **SERVINGS:** 4

This Cherry Tomato & Garlic Pasta is a delicious and nutritious high-fiber meal. Packed with vibrant cherry tomatoes and the robust flavor of garlic, it's a quick and easy recipe that's perfect for a healthy dinner.

INGREDIENTS

- 8 ounces whole-wheat penne pasta
- 2 tablespoons extra-virgin olive oil
- 6 cloves garlic, peeled
- 2 cups cherry tomatoes
- 1 medium yellow squash, halved and sliced 1/4 inch thick
- ¾ teaspoon salt
- 1 cup chopped fresh basil
- 1 cup pearl-size or mini mozzarella balls (about 4 ounces)
- ¼ cup finely grated Parmesan cheese

INGREDIENTS

1. Bring a large pot of water to a boil. Add pasta and cook according to package directions. Reserve 1/4 cup cooking water, drain the pasta and cover to keep warm.
2. Meanwhile, heat oil in a large nonstick skillet over medium-high heat. Add garlic, reduce heat to medium and cook, stirring, until it begins to soften and turn light golden, about 3 minutes.
3. Add tomatoes, squash and salt; cook, stirring occasionally, until the squash softens and the tomatoes begin to burst, 4 to 5 minutes. Lightly mash the garlic with the back of a spoon. Remove from heat.
4. Add the pasta and reserved cooking water to the pan along with basil and mozzarella; toss to combine. Serve topped with Parmesan.

Nutritional Value: 355 calories | 24g protein. | 15g fat | 49g carbohydrate | Fiber: 25g

WHOLE-WHEAT PASTA WITH LENTIL BOLOGNESE

PREP TIME: 10 MINS   **COOK TIME:** 50 MINS   **SERVINGS:** 4

This hearty and flavorful dish is a vegetarian twist on the classic Bolognese sauce. Lentils provide protein and fiber, while the whole-wheat pasta adds another layer of complexity.

INGREDIENTS

- 1 tablespoon olive oil
- 1 onion, chopped
- 2 carrots, chopped
- 2 celery stalks, chopped
- 2 cloves garlic, minced
- 1 cup dry green lentils, rinsed
- 4 cups crushed tomatoes (28-ounce can)
- 1 cup vegetable broth
- 1 tablespoon tomato paste
- 1 teaspoon dried oregano
- 1/2 teaspoon dried thyme
- Salt and freshly ground black pepper, to taste
- 9 ounces whole-wheat pasta
- Fresh basil leaves, for garnish (optional)
- Grated Parmesan cheese, for garnish (optional)

Nutritional Value: 300 calories | 25g protein. | 15g fat | 50g carbohydrate | Fiber: 21g

INGREDIENTS

1. Heat olive oil in a large pot or Dutch oven over medium heat. Add onion, carrots, and celery and cook, stirring occasionally, until softened, about 5 minutes.
2. Add garlic and cook for another minute, until fragrant.
3. Stir in lentils, crushed tomatoes, vegetable broth, tomato paste, oregano, and thyme. Season with salt and pepper to taste. Bring to a boil, then reduce heat and simmer for 20-25 minutes, or until lentils are tender and sauce has thickened slightly.
4. While the sauce simmers, cook whole-wheat pasta according to package directions. Drain and set aside. Once the sauce is finished, taste and adjust seasonings as needed.
5. To serve, toss cooked pasta with lentil Bolognese sauce. Garnish with fresh basil leaves and grated Parmesan cheese, if desired.

KALE, QUINOA & APPLE SALAD

PREP TIME: 15 MINS   **COOK TIME:** 30 MINS   **SERVINGS:** 4

This hearty and nutritious Kale, Quinoa & Apple Salad is not only packed with flavor but also high in fiber, thanks to the combination of fresh kale, quinoa, and crisp apples. It's a perfect dish for a healthy and satisfying meal.

INGREDIENTS

- 2 tablespoons cider vinegar
- 1 tablespoon pure maple syrup
- ½ teaspoon salt
- ¼ teaspoon ground pepper
- ¼ cup extra-virgin olive oil
- 1 large bunch curly kale, stemmed and thinly sliced (about 8 cups)
- 2 medium Honeycrisp or Gala apples, unpeeled, roughly chopped
- 1 medium fennel bulb, cored and thinly sliced (3 cups)
- 2 cups cooked quinoa, at room temperature or chilled
- ½ cup slivered almonds, toasted (see Tip)
- ⅓ cup dried cherries
- ¼ cup crumbled blue cheese

INGREDIENTS

1. Whisk vinegar, maple syrup, salt and pepper together in a large bowl. Slowly drizzle in oil, whisking until combined.
2. Add kale and massage into the dressing with clean hands until well coated and slightly tender, 3 to 5 minutes. Add apples, fennel and quinoa; toss until combined.
3. Divide among 4 plates and top with almonds, cherries and blue cheese.

Nutritional Value: 364 calories | 21g protein. | 17g fat | 34g carbohydrate | Fiber: 25g

SUPERFOOD CHOPPED SALAD WITH SALMON & CREAMY GARLIC DRESSING

PREP TIME: 15 MINS   **COOK TIME:** 30 MINS   **SERVINGS:** 4

Short Intro: This Superfood Chopped Salad with Salmon & Creamy Garlic Dressing is a delicious and nutritious meal that's rich in fiber. It's a wholesome option for a satisfying and healthy dinner.

INGREDIENTS

- 1 pound salmon fillet
- ½ cup low-fat plain yogurt
- ¼ cup mayonnaise
- 2 tablespoons lemon juice
- 2 tablespoons grated Parmesan cheese
- 1 tablespoon finely chopped fresh parsley
- 1 tablespoon snipped fresh chives
- 2 teaspoons reduced-sodium tamari or soy sauce
- 1 medium clove garlic, minced
- ¼ teaspoon ground pepper
- 8 cups chopped curly kale
- 2 cups chopped broccoli
- 2 cups chopped red cabbage
- 2 cups finely diced carrots
- ½ cup sunflower seeds, toasted

INGREDIENTS

1. Arrange rack in upper third of oven. Preheat broiler to high. Line a baking sheet with foil.
2. Place salmon on the prepared baking sheet, skin-side down. Broil, rotating the pan from front to back once, until the salmon is opaque in the center, 8 to 12 minutes. Cut into 4 portions.
3. Meanwhile, whisk yogurt, mayonnaise, lemon juice, Parmesan, parsley, chives, tamari (or soy sauce), garlic and pepper in a small bowl.
4. Combine kale, broccoli, cabbage, carrots and sunflower seeds in a large bowl. Add 3/4 cup of the dressing and toss to coat. Divide the salad among 4 dinner plates and top each with a piece of salmon and about 1 tablespoon of the remaining dressing.

Nutritional Value: 362 calories | 30g protein. | 17g fat | 35g carbohydrate | Fiber: 26g

GREEK SALAD WITH EDAMAME

PREP TIME: 20 MINS   **COOK TIME:** 40 MINS   **SERVINGS:** 4

This Greek Salad with Edamame is not only a delightful and refreshing dish but also a high-fiber powerhouse. Packed with beans and fresh vegetables, it's a perfect choice for a healthy and satisfying meal. Let's get started!

INGREDIENTS

- ¼ cup red-wine vinegar
- 3 tablespoons extra-virgin olive oil
- ¼ teaspoon salt
- ¼ teaspoon ground pepper
- 8 cups chopped romaine (about 2 romaine hearts)
- 16 ounces frozen shelled edamame (about 3 cups), thawed (see Tip)
- 1 cup halved cherry or grape tomatoes
- ½ European cucumber, sliced
- ½ cup crumbled feta cheese
- ¼ cup slivered fresh basil
- ¼ cup sliced Kalamata olives
- ¼ cup slivered red onion

INGREDIENTS

1. Whisk vinegar, oil, salt and pepper in a large bowl.
2. Add romaine, edamame, tomatoes, cucumber, feta, basil, olives and onion; toss to coat.

Nutritional Value: 344 calories | 25g protein. | 14g fat | 33g carbohydrate | Fiber: 26g

GODDESS VEGGIE BOWLS WITH CHICKEN

PREP TIME: 15 MINS   **COOK TIME:** 45 MINS   **SERVINGS:** 4

These Goddess Veggie Bowls with Chicken are a flavor-packed and healthy lunch option. Marinated chicken combines with a creamy herb dressing and a variety of fresh vegetables for a satisfying and colorful meal.

INGREDIENTS

- ½ cup low-fat buttermilk½ cup low-fat plain Greek yogurt
- ¼ cup lightly packed fresh flat-leaf parsley
- 1 tablespoon chopped fresh chives
- 1 tablespoon lemon juice plus 2 tsp. lemon zest, divided
- 1 clove garlic, peeled
- 1 ¼ pounds chicken tenders
- 1 ⅓ cups water
- ⅔ cup quinoa, rinsed
- ⅛ teaspoon salt
- 4 cups lacinato (dinosaur) kale, stems trimmed, thinly sliced
- ½ medium cucumber, sliced
- 2 bell peppers, preferably 1 red and 1 orange or yellow, diced
- 1 pint cherry tomatoes, halved if large
- 1 avocado, cubed or sliced
- ½ cup shredded sharp Cheddar cheese
- ¼ cup sliced almonds, toasted

INGREDIENTS

1. Combine buttermilk, yogurt, parsley, chives, lemon juice and garlic in a food processor and blend until smooth. Refrigerate 1/2 cup to use as dressing. Pour the remaining mixture into a large, sealable plastic bag and add chicken tenders.
2. Remove air from the bag, seal it and marinate in the refrigerator for at least 4 hours (and up to 6 hours).
3. Combine water and quinoa in a medium saucepan; bring to a boil over medium heat. Reduce heat to medium-low, cover and simmer until the quinoa is tender, 13 to 15 minutes. Drain any excess liquid. Add lemon zest and salt; fluff with a fork.
4. Meanwhile, position oven rack about 4 inches from heat source; preheat broiler. Line a large rimmed baking sheet with foil. Coat with cooking spray. Remove the chicken from the marinade, shaking off excess (discard marinade), and place on the prepared baking sheet.
5. Broil the chicken, flipping once, until an instant-read thermometer inserted in the center registers 165°F, 8 to 12 minutes. Add kale and 1/4 cup of the reserved dressing to the quinoa; stir to combine. Divide the quinoa mixture among 4 bowls.
6. Top with cucumber, bell peppers, tomatoes and chicken. Drizzle the remaining 1/4 cup dressing over the bowls. Top with avocado, cheese and almonds.

Nutritional Value: 350 calories | 25g protein. | 19g fat | 35g carbohydrate | Fiber: 24g

BLACK BEAN AND CORN SALAD

PREP TIME: 15 MINS **COOK TIME:** 25 MINS **SERVINGS:** 4

This Black Bean and Corn Salad is a refreshing and high-fiber dish that's perfect for a light and healthy meal. Packed with beans and fresh vegetables, it's a great choice for a quick and satisfying side dish or even a main course.

INGREDIENTS

- 2 cans (15 ounces each) black beans, drained and rinsed
- 2 cups frozen corn, thawed
- 1 red bell pepper, diced
- 1/2 red onion, finely chopped
- 1 cup cherry tomatoes, halved
- 1/4 cup fresh cilantro, chopped
- 1/4 cup extra-virgin olive oil
- 2 tablespoons fresh lime juice
- 1 teaspoon ground cumin
- Salt and pepper to taste
- Optional: diced avocado for garnish

INGREDIENTS

1. In a large bowl, combine the black beans, corn, red bell pepper, red onion, cherry tomatoes, and cilantro.
2. In a small bowl, whisk together the olive oil, lime juice, ground cumin, salt, and pepper.
3. Pour the dressing over the bean and vegetable mixture. Toss everything together to ensure even coating.
4. Taste and adjust the seasoning if needed. If desired, garnish the salad with diced avocado.
5. Serve immediately or refrigerate for a few hours to let the flavors meld

Nutritional Value: 320 calories | 24g protein. | 12g fat | 37g carbohydrate | Fiber: 27g

QUINOA AND BLACK BEAN STUFFED PEPPERS

PREP TIME: 20 MINS   **COOK TIME:** 40 MINS   **SERVINGS:** 4

Quinoa and Black Bean Stuffed Peppers are a delicious and nutritious dish packed with fiber, thanks to the combination of quinoa and black beans. These stuffed peppers make for a wholesome and satisfying meal.

INGREDIENTS

- 4 large bell peppers (any color)
- 1 cup quinoa, uncooked
- 2 cups vegetable broth
- 1 can (15 oz) black beans, drained and rinsed
- 1 cup corn kernels (fresh or frozen)
- 1 cup diced tomatoes (canned or fresh)
- 1/2 cup diced red onion
- 2 cloves garlic, minced
- 1 teaspoon chili powder
- 1/2 teaspoon cumin
- 1/2 teaspoon paprika
- Salt and pepper to taste
- 1 cup shredded cheddar cheese (optional, for topping)
- Fresh cilantro, for garnish

INGREDIENTS

1. Preheat your oven to 375°F (190°C). Wash the bell peppers, cut the tops off, and remove the seeds and membranes. Set them aside in a baking dish.
2. In a medium-sized saucepan, combine the quinoa and vegetable broth. Bring to a boil, then reduce the heat to low, cover, and simmer for about 15-20 minutes, or until the quinoa is cooked and the liquid is absorbed.
3. Fluff the quinoa with a fork and set it aside. In a large skillet, heat some olive oil over medium heat. Add the diced red onion and garlic, and sauté until they become translucent.
4. Stir in the black beans, corn, diced tomatoes, chili powder, cumin, paprika, salt, and pepper. Cook for 5-7 minutes until the mixture is heated through.
5. Combine the cooked quinoa with the black bean mixture, and mix thoroughly. Carefully stuff each bell pepper with the quinoa and black bean mixture, filling them to the top.
6. If desired, sprinkle shredded cheddar cheese on top of each stuffed pepper. Place the stuffed peppers in the baking dish and cover with aluminum foil.
7. Bake for 25-30 minutes, or until the peppers are tender and the cheese is melted and bubbly.
8. Remove from the oven and let them cool for a few minutes before serving.
9. Garnish with fresh cilantro and serve your Quinoa and Black Bean Stuffed Peppers hot.

Nutritional Value: 350 calories | 26g protein. | 12g fat | 34g carbohydrate | Fiber: 26g

BEAN BURRITOS

PREP TIME: 10 MINS   **COOK TIME:** 30 MINS   **SERVINGS:** 4

Bean burritos are a delicious and satisfying dish filled with beans, salsa, cooked rice, and melted cheddar cheese, all wrapped in a warm flour tortilla. They are easy to make and perfect for a quick and flavorful meal.

INGREDIENTS

- 1 can (16 ounces) vegetarian refried beans
- 1 cup salsa
- 1 cup cooked long grain rice
- 2 cups shredded cheddar cheese, divided
- 12 flour tortillas (6 inches)
- Shredded lettuce, optional

INGREDIENTS

1. Preheat oven to 375°. In a large bowl, combine beans, salsa, rice and 1 cup cheese.
2. Spoon about 1/3 cup mixture off-center on each tortilla. Fold the sides and ends over filling and roll up.
3. Arrange burritos in a greased 13x9-in. baking dish. Sprinkle with remaining 1 cup cheese.
4. Cover and bake until heated through, 20-25 minutes. If desired, top with lettuce.

Nutritional Value: 350 calories | 26g protein. | 12g fat | 34g carbohydrate | Fiber: 25g

MINESTRONE WITH TURKEY

PREP TIME: 10 MINS **COOK TIME:** 30 MINS **SERVINGS:** 6

Minestrone with Turkey is a hearty and nutritious soup filled with fiber-rich ingredients, making it a delicious and healthy choice for any meal. Packed with flavorful vegetables, tender turkey, and comforting broth, this dish is sure to satisfy your taste buds.

INGREDIENTS

- 1 tablespoon olive oil
- 1 medium onion, chopped
- 1 medium carrot, sliced
- 1 celery rib, sliced
- 1 garlic clove, minced
- 4 cups chicken broth or homemade turkey stock
- 1 can (14-1/2 ounces) diced tomatoes, undrained
- 2/3 cup each frozen peas, corn and cut green beans, thawed
- 1/2 cup uncooked elbow macaroni
- 1 teaspoon salt
- 1/4 teaspoon dried basil
- 1/4 teaspoon dried oregano
- 1/4 teaspoon pepper
- 1 bay leaf
- 1 cup cubed cooked turkey
- 1 small zucchini, halved lengthwise and cut into 1/4-inch slices
- 1/4 cup grated Parmesan cheese, optional

Nutritional Value: 323 calories | 28g protein. | 17g fat | 37g carbohydrate | Fiber: 25g

INGREDIENTS

1. In a Dutch oven, heat oil over medium-high heat. Add onion, carrot and celery; cook and stir until tender. Add garlic; cook 1 minute longer. Add broth, vegetables, macaroni and seasonings. Bring to a boil.
2. Reduce heat; simmer, uncovered, 5 minutes or until macaroni is al dente. Stir in turkey and zucchini; cook until zucchini is crisp-tender. Discard bay leaf. If desired, sprinkle servings with cheese.
3. Freeze option: Transfer cooled soup to freezer container and freeze up to 3 months.
4. To use, thaw in the refrigerator overnight. Transfer to a saucepan. Cover and cook over medium heat until heated through. Serve with cheese if desired.

SPINACH AND MUSHROOM QUESADILLAS

PREP TIME: 15 MINS   **COOK TIME:** 30 MINS   **SERVINGS:** 2

Boost your daily fiber intake with these nutritious and delicious high-fiber recipes. Fiber is essential for a healthy digestive system and can aid in weight management. Try out our Spinach and Mushroom Quesadillas recipe for a satisfying and fiber-rich meal.

INGREDIENTS

- 2 whole wheat tortillas
- 1 cup fresh spinach, washed and chopped
- 1 cup mushrooms, sliced
- 1/2 cup shredded low-fat mozzarella cheese
- 1/4 cup diced red bell pepper
- 1/4 cup diced red onion
- 1 clove garlic, minced
- 1/2 teaspoon olive oil
- Salt and pepper to taste

INGREDIENTS

1. Heat olive oil in a large skillet over medium heat. Add minced garlic and sauté for a minute until fragrant.
2. Add the sliced mushrooms, diced red bell pepper, and diced red onion to the skillet. Cook for 5-6 minutes until the mushrooms are tender and the vegetables have softened. Season with salt and pepper to taste.
3. Place a tortilla in a clean, dry skillet over medium heat. Sprinkle half of the shredded mozzarella cheese evenly over the tortilla.
4. Spread half of the sautéed mushroom and vegetable mixture on top of the cheese.
5. Add half of the chopped spinach on top of the vegetables. Place the second tortilla on top to create a quesadilla. Press down gently with a spatula. Cook for 2-3 minutes on each side, or until the tortillas are golden brown and the cheese has melted.
6. Remove the quesadilla from the skillet and let it cool for a minute before cutting it into wedges.
7. Repeat the process with the remaining ingredients to make the second quesadilla.
8. Serve your Spinach and Mushroom Quesadillas hot, and enjoy a high-fiber, nutritious meal.

Nutritional Value: 320 calories | 21g protein. | 13g fat | 34g carbohydrate | Fiber: 25g

CREAMY LENTIL CURRY WITH ROASTED BUTTERNUT SQUASH

PREP TIME: 15 MINS **COOK TIME:** 30 MINS **SERVINGS:** 4

Indulge in the wholesome goodness of this Creamy Lentil Curry with Roasted Butternut Squash, a high-fiber dish that's as delicious as it is nutritious. This recipe is a great way to boost your daily fiber intake while enjoying a satisfying meal.

INGREDIENTS

For the Roasted Butternut Squash:
- 1 medium butternut squash, peeled, seeded, and cut into 1-inch cubes
- 2 tablespoons olive oil
- 1 teaspoon ground cumin
- 1 teaspoon ground coriander
- Salt and pepper to taste

For the Lentil Curry:
- 1 cup dried brown or green lentils, rinsed and drained
- 1 tablespoon olive oil
- 1 onion, finely chopped
- 3 cloves garlic, minced
- 1 tablespoon fresh ginger, minced
- 1 tablespoon curry powder
- 1 teaspoon ground turmeric
- 1 teaspoon ground cumin
- 1 teaspoon ground coriander
- 1 can (14 oz) diced tomatoes
- 1 can (14 oz) coconut milk
- Salt and pepper to taste
- Fresh cilantro leaves for garnish

Nutritional Value: 400 calories | 25g protein. | 20g fat | 35g carbohydrate | Fiber: 25g

INGREDIENTS

1. Preheat your oven to 400°F (200°C). In a large bowl, toss the butternut squash cubes with olive oil, ground cumin, ground coriander, salt, and pepper.
2. Spread the seasoned squash on a baking sheet and roast in the preheated oven for about 20-25 minutes or until they are tender and slightly caramelized. Set aside.
3. In a large saucepan, heat 1 tablespoon of olive oil over medium heat. Add the chopped onion and sauté for about 3-4 minutes until it becomes translucent.
4. Stir in the minced garlic and ginger, and cook for an additional minute until fragrant.
5. Add the curry powder, turmeric, ground cumin, and ground coriander to the onion mixture. Cook for 2 minutes, stirring constantly to release the flavors.
6. Add the rinsed lentils to the pan and stir to coat them with the spice mixture.
7. Pour in the diced tomatoes and coconut milk. Bring the mixture to a gentle simmer, then reduce the heat and let it cook for about 15-20 minutes, or until the lentils are tender and the sauce thickens. Season with salt and pepper to taste.
8. Serve the creamy lentil curry over cooked rice or your favorite grain, topped with the roasted butternut squash cubes and fresh cilantro leaves.

ROASTED BEET AND CHICKPEA SALAD

PREP TIME: 15 MINS **COOK TIME:** 45 MINS **SERVINGS:** 4

This Roasted Beet and Chickpea Salad is a delightful combination of earthy roasted beets, crispy chickpeas, and fresh greens. It's a nutritious and flavorful choice for a healthy meal.

INGREDIENTS

- 3 medium beets, peeled and cut into 1-inch cubes
- 1 can (15 oz) chickpeas, drained and rinsed
- 2 tablespoons olive oil
- 1 teaspoon ground cumin
- 1/2 teaspoon paprika
- Salt and pepper to taste
- 6 cups mixed greens (e.g., spinach, arugula, or kale)
- 1/4 cup crumbled feta cheese
- 1/4 cup chopped walnuts
- 1/4 cup balsamic vinaigrette dressing

INGREDIENTS

1. Preheat your oven to 400°F (200°C). In a large mixing bowl, combine the cubed beets, chickpeas, olive oil, ground cumin, paprika, salt, and pepper. Toss everything together until the beets and chickpeas are evenly coated with the seasonings and oil.
2. Spread the beet and chickpea mixture on a baking sheet lined with parchment paper. Roast in the preheated oven for about 35-40 minutes, or until the beets are tender and the chickpeas are crispy, stirring once halfway through.
3. While the beets and chickpeas are roasting, prepare your salad. Divide the mixed greens among four serving plates.
4. Once the roasted beets and chickpeas are ready, remove them from the oven and let them cool for a few minutes.
5. Arrange the roasted beet and chickpea mixture over the greens on each plate. Sprinkle each salad with crumbled feta cheese and chopped walnuts.
6. Drizzle the balsamic vinaigrette dressing over the top.
Serve immediately and enjoy your high-fiber Roasted Beet and Chickpea Salad!

Nutritional Value: 320 calories | 21g protein. | 18g fat | 32g carbohydrate | Fiber: 25g

EGGPLANT AND ZUCCHINI RATATOUILLE

PREP TIME: 20 MINS **COOK TIME:** 40 MINS **SERVINGS:** 4

This Eggplant and Zucchini Ratatouille is a delightful, fiber-packed dish that's not only delicious but also healthy. Packed with a variety of vegetables and spices, it's a perfect choice for those looking to increase their daily fiber intake.

INGREDIENTS

- 1 large eggplant, diced
- 2 medium zucchinis, diced
- 1 red bell pepper, diced
- 1 yellow bell pepper, diced
- 1 onion, finely chopped
- 3 cloves of garlic, minced
- 1 can (14 oz) diced tomatoes (with juices)
- 2 tablespoons olive oil
- 1 teaspoon dried thyme
- 1 teaspoon dried oregano
- 1/2 teaspoon red pepper flakes (adjust to taste)
- Salt and pepper to taste
- Fresh basil leaves, for garnish

INGREDIENTS

1. Start by preparing the eggplant. Place the diced eggplant in a colander, sprinkle with salt, and let it sit for about 15 minutes. This will help draw out excess moisture and reduce bitterness.
2. After 15 minutes, rinse the eggplant under cold water and pat it dry with paper towels.
3. In a large skillet or frying pan, heat the olive oil over medium heat. Add the chopped onion and minced garlic, and sauté until they become fragrant and translucent.
4. Add the diced red and yellow bell peppers to the skillet. Cook for about 5 minutes, until they start to soften.
5. Stir in the diced zucchini and eggplant. Cook for another 5-7 minutes, or until the vegetables are slightly tender and start to brown.
6. Add the can of diced tomatoes with their juices, dried thyme, dried oregano, and red pepper flakes. Stir well to combine all the ingredients.
7. Reduce the heat to low, cover the skillet, and let the ratatouille simmer for 15-20 minutes, stirring occasionally. The vegetables should be soft and the flavors well combined.
8. Season with salt and pepper to taste. Serve the Eggplant and Zucchini Ratatouille hot, garnished with fresh basil leaves.

Nutritional Value: 250 calories | 25g protein. | 7g fat | 34g carbohydrate | Fiber: 25g

SWEET POTATO AND BLACK BEAN TACOS

PREP TIME: 15 MINS   **COOK TIME:** 30 MINS   **SERVINGS:** 4

These Sweet Potato and Black Bean Tacos are a delicious and nutritious twist on traditional tacos. These tacos are not only satisfying but also great for your digestive health.

INGREDIENTS

- 2 medium sweet potatoes, peeled and diced
- 1 can (15 oz) black beans, drained and rinsed
- 1 red onion, finely chopped
- 2 cloves garlic, minced
- 1 teaspoon ground cumin
- 1 teaspoon chili powder
- 1/2 teaspoon paprika
- Salt and pepper to taste
- 1 tablespoon olive oil
- 8 small whole wheat tortillas
- 1 cup shredded lettuce
- 1 cup diced tomatoes
- 1/2 cup diced red bell pepper
- 1/2 cup shredded cheddar cheese (optional)
- 1/2 cup plain Greek yogurt (optional)
- Fresh cilantro for garnish (optional)

Nutritional Value: 350 calories | 21g protein. | 12g fat | 44g carbohydrate | Fiber: 24g

INGREDIENTS

1. In a large skillet, heat the olive oil over medium heat. Add the chopped red onion and cook for 2-3 minutes until it becomes translucent.
2. Add the diced sweet potatoes to the skillet and cook for about 15 minutes, or until they are tender and slightly crispy, stirring occasionally.
3. Stir in the minced garlic, ground cumin, chili powder, paprika, salt, and pepper.
4. Cook for an additional 2 minutes to toast the spices.
5. Add the black beans to the skillet and cook for 3-4 minutes, or until they are heated through. Mash some of the beans with a fork to create a creamy texture.
6. Warm the whole wheat tortillas in a dry skillet or microwave according to the package instructions.
7. Assemble your tacos: Place a generous spoonful of the sweet potato and black bean mixture onto each tortilla. Top with shredded lettuce, diced tomatoes, diced red bell pepper, and, if desired, shredded cheddar cheese.
8. Drizzle with plain Greek yogurt and garnish with fresh cilantro if you like.

BROCCOLI AND CHEDDAR STUFFED BAKED POTATOES

PREP TIME: 20 MINS   **COOK TIME:** 40 MINS   **SERVINGS:** 4

These Broccoli and Cheddar Stuffed Baked Potatoes are a delicious and nutritious way to increase your fiber intake. Packed with flavor and nutrients, they make a satisfying and wholesome meal.

INGREDIENTS

- 4 large russet potatoes
- 2 cups broccoli florets
- 1 cup shredded cheddar cheese
- 1/2 cup sour cream
- 2 tablespoons butter
- 1/4 cup chopped green onions
- Salt and pepper to taste

INGREDIENTS

1. Preheat your oven to 400°F (200°C). Wash and scrub the potatoes thoroughly. Pierce each potato a few times with a fork, and then place them directly on the oven rack. Bake for about 45-60 minutes, or until the potatoes are tender and the skin is crisp.
2. While the potatoes are baking, steam or boil the broccoli florets until they are tender but still crisp, usually for about 4-5 minutes. Drain and set aside.
3. Once the potatoes are done, remove them from the oven and let them cool for a few minutes. Slice off the top 1/3 of each potato and scoop out the flesh, leaving a potato shell about 1/4-inch thick.
4. In a large mixing bowl, combine the scooped-out potato flesh, steamed broccoli, 3/4 of the shredded cheddar cheese, sour cream, butter, and green onions.
5. Mix well until all the ingredients are evenly combined. Season with salt and pepper to taste.
6. Stuff each potato shell with the broccoli and cheddar mixture, and top with the remaining cheddar cheese.
7. Return the stuffed potatoes to the oven and bake for an additional 15-20 minutes, or until the cheese is melted and bubbly, and the potatoes are heated through.
8. Once done, remove from the oven, let them cool for a couple of minutes, and serve hot.

Nutritional Value: 350 calories | 25g protein. | 15g fat | 43g carbohydrate | Fiber: 25g

VEGAN LENTIL AND VEGETABLE STIR-FRY

PREP TIME: 15 MINS **COOK TIME:** 20 MINS **SERVINGS:** 4

This Vegan Lentil and Vegetable Stir-Fry is a delightful and nutritious dish that's not only high in fiber but also packed with flavor. It's perfect for a quick and healthy weeknight meal.

INGREDIENTS

- 1 cup dry brown lentils
- 2 cups water
- 2 tablespoons vegetable oil
- 1 onion, chopped
- 3 cloves garlic, minced
- 1 red bell pepper, sliced
- 1 yellow bell pepper, sliced
- 2 cups broccoli florets
- 1 cup snap peas, trimmed
- 1 carrot, thinly sliced
- 1/4 cup low-sodium soy sauce
- 2 tablespoons rice vinegar
- 1 tablespoon maple syrup or agave nectar
- 1 teaspoon ginger, minced
- 1 teaspoon red pepper flakes (adjust to your spice preference)
- Salt and pepper, to taste
- 2 cups cooked brown rice or quinoa, for serving

Nutritional Value: 340 calories | 25g protein. | 14g fat | 34g carbohydrate | Fiber: 24g

INGREDIENTS

1. Rinse the lentils under cold water, then place them in a medium-sized saucepan. Add 2 cups of water and bring to a boil.
2. Reduce heat to low, cover, and simmer for about 20-25 minutes or until the lentils are tender but not mushy. Drain any excess water and set aside. In a large skillet or wok, heat the vegetable oil over medium-high heat. Add the chopped onion and garlic, sauté for 2-3 minutes until fragrant and slightly softened.
3. Add the sliced red and yellow bell peppers, broccoli florets, snap peas, and carrot to the skillet. Stir-fry for about 5-7 minutes until the vegetables are tender-crisp.
4. In a small bowl, whisk together the soy sauce, rice vinegar, maple syrup (or agave nectar), minced ginger, and red pepper flakes.
5. Add the cooked lentils to the skillet and pour the sauce over the vegetables and lentils. Stir well to combine and cook for an additional 2-3 minutes to heat everything through.
6. Season with salt and pepper to taste. Serve the Vegan Lentil and Vegetable Stir-Fry over cooked brown rice or quinoa. Garnish with fresh cilantro or green onions if desired.

SPICY CHORIZO-AND-PINTO BEAN CHILI

PREP TIME: 20 MINS **COOK TIME:** 40 MINS **SERVINGS:** 4

Get ready to spice up your taste buds with this flavorful Spicy Chorizo-and-Pinto Bean Chili. Packed with fiber, protein, and a kick of heat, it's the perfect dish for a chilly evening.

INGREDIENTS

- 1 tablespoon olive oil
- 12 ounces fresh Mexican chorizo, casings removed
- 1 yellow onion, chopped
- 1 poblano chile, stemmed, seeded, and chopped
- 1 tablespoon tomato paste
- 2 teaspoon chili powder
- 1 teaspoon kosher salt
- 1 teaspoon ground cumin
- 1 teaspoon garlic powder
- 2 15-ounce cans no-salt-added pinto beans, drained and rinsed
- 3 cups unsalted chicken broth
- diced avocado, finely shredded cabbage, chopped fresh cilantro, and lime wedges, for serving

INGREDIENTS

1. Heat oil in a large pot over medium-high. Add chorizo in large chunks; cook until browned, about 2 minutes.
2. Break up chorizo with a wooden spoon. Cook, stirring occasionally, until browned on all sides, about 3 minutes.
3. Transfer to a bowl using a slotted spoon. Discard all but 1 tablespoon drippings in pot.
4. Add onion and poblano to pot; cook, stirring often, until softened, about 5 minutes. Add tomato paste, chili powder, salt, cumin, and garlic powder; cook, stirring constantly, until fragrant, about 1 minute. Add 1 cup beans and mash with a fork.
5. Add broth, chorizo, and remaining beans; bring to a boil. Reduce heat to medium-low and simmer until slightly thickened, about 5 minutes. Top with avocado, cabbage, and cilantro.
Serve with lime wedges.

Nutritional Value: 324 calories | 22g protein. | 14g fat | 35g carbohydrate | Fiber: 25g

SLOW-COOKER BLACK BEAN AND SPINACH ENCHILADAS

PREP TIME: 20 MINS   **COOK TIME:** 60 MINS   **SERVINGS:** 4

A wholesome and satisfying dish with the goodness of black beans and spinach, slow-cooked to perfection and wrapped in a warm tortilla.

INGREDIENTS

- 1 15.5-ounce can black beans, rinsed
- 1 10-ounce package frozen chopped spinach, thawed and squeezed of excess liquid
- 1 cup frozen corn
- ½ teaspoon ground cumin
- 8 ounces sharp Cheddar, grated (2 cups)
- kosher salt and black pepper
- 2 16-ounce jars salsa (3 1/2 cups)
- 8 6-inch corn tortillas, warmed
  1 medium head romaine lettuce, chopped (6 cups)
- 4 radishes, cut into matchsticks
  ½ cup grape tomatoes, halved
- ½ cucumber, halved and sliced
- 3 tablespoons fresh lime juice
- 2 tablespoons olive oil
- sliced scallions, for serving

Nutritional Value: 340 calories | 26g protein. | 12g fat | 34g carbohydrate | Fiber: 24g

INGREDIENTS

1. In a medium bowl, mash half the beans. Add the spinach, corn, cumin, 1 cup of the Cheddar, the remaining beans, ½ teaspoon salt, and ¼ teaspoon pepper and mix to combine.
2. Spread 1 jar of the salsa in the bottom of a 4- to 6-quart slow cooker. Dividing evenly, roll up the bean mixture in the tortillas (about ½ cup each) and place the rolls seam-side down in a single layer in the slow cooker. Top with the remaining salsa and Cheddar.
3. Cover and cook until heated through, on low for 2½ to 3 hours. Before serving, toss the lettuce, radishes, tomatoes, and cucumber in a large bowl with the lime juice, oil, and ½ teaspoon each salt and pepper. Serve with the enchiladas and sprinkle with the scallions.

GLAZED BRUSSELS SPROUTS ON OLIVE OIL-FRIED BREAD

PREP TIME: 20 MINS   **COOK TIME:** 40 MINS   **SERVINGS:** 4

A delightful combination of crispy Brussels sprouts glazed in a savory sauce, served atop crispy olive oil-fried bread, bringing a burst of flavor and texture to your plate.

INGREDIENTS

- 5 tablespoons olive oil, divided
- 1 1-lb. ciabatta loaf (12 by 7 in.), split horizontally
- 2 cloves garlic
- 1 ¼ teaspoons kosher salt, divided
- 1 pound fresh Brussels sprouts, trimmed and halved
- ½ cup pomegranate juice
- ¼ cup balsamic vinegar
- 1 1-lb. container whole-milk ricotta cheese
- ¾ cup toasted, chopped hazelnuts
- chopped fresh flat-leaf parsley and freshly ground black pepper, for serving

INGREDIENTS

1. Preheat oven to 225°F. Heat 2 tablespoons oil in a large cast-iron or other heavy skillet over medium. (Trim bread to fit skillet if necessary.) Place 1 bread half, cut side down, in skillet.
2. Fry, occasionally pressing down middle with a spatula, until golden, 3 to 4 minutes. Transfer bread, cut side up, to a baking sheet. Repeat with 1 tablespoon oil and remaining bread half. Remove skillet from heat. Rub cut sides of bread generously with garlic; season with ¼ teaspoon salt. Transfer baking sheet to oven to keep bread warm.
3. Add remaining 2 tablespoons oil to skillet over medium. Carefully add Brussels sprouts, mostly cut side down, and cook, undisturbed, until golden brown, 4 to 5 minutes.
4. Season with ¼ teaspoon salt and toss. Cook, undisturbed, until golden in parts, 4 to 5 minutes. Add pomegranate juice, vinegar, and ½ teaspoon salt; stir to coat. Bring to a simmer over medium.
5. Reduce heat to medium-low; simmer, stirring often, until Brussels sprouts are tender and liquid reduces to a glaze, 15 to 18 minutes. Stir ricotta and remaining ¼ teaspoon salt in a small bowl. Spread over cut sides of bread.
6. Top with Brussels sprouts, hazelnuts, parsley, and several grinds of pepper. Cut each bread half into 4 pieces.

Nutritional Value: 340 calories | 21g protein. | 15g fat | 30g carbohydrate | Fiber: 24g

CAULIFLOWER AND CHICKPEA STEW WITH COUSCOUS

PREP TIME: 20 MINS   **COOK TIME:** 40 MINS   **SERVINGS:** 4

This hearty Cauliflower and Chickpea Stew With Couscous is a delicious and nutritious meal that's high in fiber and packed with flavor.

INGREDIENTS

- 2 tablespoons olive oil
- 1 medium onion, chopped
- 1 ½ teaspoons ground cumin
- ½ teaspoon ground ginger
- kosher salt and black pepper
- 1 28-ounce can whole tomatoes
- 1 15-ounce can chickpeas, rinsed
- 1 head cauliflower, cored and cut into small florets
- ½ cup raisins
- 1 5-ounce package baby spinach, chopped
- 1 cup couscous

INGREDIENTS

1. Heat the oil in a large saucepan over medium heat. Add the onion and cook, stirring occasionally, until it starts to soften, 4 to 5 minutes.
2. Add the cumin, ginger, ½ teaspoon salt, and ¼ teaspoon pepper and cook, stirring, until fragrant, 1 minute.
3. Add the tomatoes (crushing with your hands as you add them) and their liquid, chickpeas, cauliflower, raisins, and ½ cup water and bring to a boil.
4. Reduce heat and simmer until the vegetables are tender and the liquid has slightly thickened, 15 to 20 minutes.
5. Fold in the spinach and cook until just wilted, 1 to 2 minutes. Meanwhile, place the couscous in a large bowl.
6. Add 1 cup of hot tap water, cover, and let sit for 5 minutes. Fluff with a fork. Serve with the stew.

Nutritional Value: 370 calories | 21g protein. | 9g fat | 32g carbohydrate | Fiber: 24g

KALE SALAD WITH ROASTED SWEET POTATO & BLACK BEANS

PREP TIME: 20 MINS   **COOK TIME:** 45 MINS   **SERVINGS:** 4

This vibrant Kale Salad with Roasted Sweet Potato & Black Beans is a delicious, nutrient-packed dish that's sure to satisfy your taste buds and keep you feeling full and energized. Packed with fiber and a medley of flavors, it's a perfect addition to your healthy recipe collection.

INGREDIENTS

- 1 large sweet potato, cut into 1/2-inch-thick wedges
- 5 tablespoons extra-virgin olive oil, divided
- 2 teaspoons ancho chile powder
- ½ teaspoon salt, divided
- 6 medium shallots, peeled and quartered
- 3 tablespoons lemon juice
- 1 large clove garlic, grated
- 1 pound kale, stemmed and torn
- 1 (15 ounce) can no-salt-added black beans, rinsed
- 1 cup cooked quinoa
- ½ cup crumbled feta cheese
- ½ cup unsalted pepitas, toasted

INGREDIENTS

1. Position racks in upper and lower thirds of oven; preheat to 425°F. Toss sweet potato with 1 tablespoon oil, chile powder and 1/8 teaspoon salt on a large rimmed baking sheet.
2. Toss shallots with 1 tablespoon oil and 1/8 teaspoon salt on another large rimmed baking sheet. Roast the vegetables, flipping once, until tender and caramelized, about 20 minutes.
3. Meanwhile, whisk lemon juice and garlic with the remaining 3 tablespoons oil and 1/4 teaspoon salt in a large bowl.
4. Add kale and massage with the dressing until bright green and shiny and the volume is reduced by about half.
5. Add beans, quinoa, feta, pepitas and the shallots. Toss to combine and serve topped with the sweet potato.

Nutritional Value: 340 calories | 21g protein. | 15g fat | 30g carbohydrate | Fiber: 24g

SPRING VEGETABLE MINESTRA WITH MINT & BASIL PISTOU

PREP TIME: 30 MINS　　**COOK TIME:** 60 MINS　　**SERVINGS:** 3

This Spring Vegetable Minestra is a delightful and nutritious dish, featuring fresh spring vegetables and a vibrant Mint & Basil Pistou. It's packed with flavor and fiber, making it a healthy and satisfying meal.

INGREDIENTS

- Soup
- 2 quarts cold water
- 2 stalks fennel plus 1/2 cup diced fennel bulb, divided
- 2 bay leaves
- 1 small bunch fresh thyme
- ½ teaspoon black peppercorns
- 2 3-inch pieces orange zest
- 8 ounces Parmesan cheese rinds
- 1 cup diced tomato
- ½ cup diced carrot
- ½ cup diced green beans
- ½ cup diced leek
- 1 (15 ounce) can no-salt-added white beans, rinsed
- ¼ teaspoon crushed red pepper
- 6 cups chopped escarole
- 4 cups spinach, stemmed
- ½ teaspoon kosher salt
- ½ teaspoon ground pepper
- Pistou
- 3 cups lightly packed basil leaves
- 1 cup lightly packed mint leaves
- ¾ cup grated Parmesan cheese
- 2 teaspoons chopped garlic
- ¼ teaspoon crushed red pepper
- ¼ cup extra-virgin olive oil

Nutritional Value: 300 calories | 21g protein. | 12g fat | 24g carbohydrate | Fiber: 21g

INGREDIENTS

1. To prepare soup: Bring water to a boil in a large pot over medium-high heat. Wrap fennel stalks, bay leaves, thyme, peppercorns and orange zest in cheesecloth and tie with kitchen string.
2. Add to the pot along with Parmesan rinds. Adjust heat to maintain a simmer, partially cover and cook for 30 minutes.
3. Stir in diced fennel, tomato, carrot, green beans, leek, white beans and crushed red pepper. Partially cover and simmer until the vegetables are very tender, about 30 minutes.
4. Meanwhile, prepare pistou: Combine basil, mint, grated Parmesan, garlic and crushed red pepper in a food processor. Process until the herbs are finely chopped.
5. Scrape down the sides. With the motor running, stream in oil and process until mostly smooth. Remove the Parmesan rinds and sachet from the soup.
6. Stir in escarole and spinach; cook until wilted, about 5 minutes. Season with salt and pepper. Serve topped with the pistou.

CHEESY MARINARA BEANS

PREP TIME: 20 MINS   **COOK TIME:** 40 MINS   **SERVINGS:** 4

These Cheesy Marinara Beans are a delicious and nutritious dish that's rich in fiber and flavor. It's a quick and easy recipe that's perfect for a wholesome meal or a flavorful side dish. With a cheesy twist on classic marinara beans, this recipe is sure to satisfy your taste buds.

INGREDIENTS

- 2 tablespoons extra-virgin olive oil
- 1 medium onion, chopped
- 2 cloves garlic, minced
- ⅓ cup tomato paste
- ¼ cup dry white wine
- 1 28-ounce can no-salt-added whole peeled tomatoes, preferably San Marzano
- 3 cups cooked corona beans or two 15-ounce cans no-salt-added cannellini beans, rinsed
- 2 tablespoons chopped fresh basil, plus more for garnish
- 2 tablespoons chopped fresh oregano, plus more for garnish
- 2 tablespoons chopped fresh parsley, plus more for garnish
- 1 large egg, lightly beaten
- ⅔ cup whole-milk ricotta cheese
- ½ cup grated Parmesan cheese, divided
- 1 cup shredded fontina cheese

INGREDIENTS

1. Heat oil in a large broiler-safe skillet over medium-high heat. Add onion and cook, stirring occasionally, until softened, about 5 minutes. Add garlic and cook, stirring, until fragrant, about 1 minute.
2. Add tomato paste and cook, stirring, until it starts to darken, about 2 minutes.
3. Add wine and cook, scraping up any browned bits, until thickened, about 1 minute. Add tomatoes and their juice, crushing the tomatoes with your hand as you add them.
4. Stir in beans, basil, oregano and parsley. Bring to a simmer. Reduce heat to maintain a simmer and cook, stirring occasionally, until thickened, 18 to 20 minutes.
5. Meanwhile, place rack in upper third of oven; preheat broiler to high. Combine egg, ricotta and 1/4 cup Parmesan in a small bowl.
6. Gently stir the ricotta mixture into the bean mixture. Sprinkle fontina and the remaining 1/4 cup Parmesan on top. Broil until the cheese is melted, 2 to 3 minutes. Garnish with more herbs, if desired.

Nutritional Value: 340 calories | 26g protein. | 18g fat | 30g carbohydrate | Fiber: 25g

JACKFRUIT BARBACOA BURRITO BOWLS

PREP TIME: 10 MINS **COOK TIME:** 30 MINS **SERVINGS:** 4

Enjoy a burst of flavors with these Jackfruit Barbacoa Burrito Bowls. Packed with fiber and protein, this plant-based delight is perfect for a hearty and healthy meal.

INGREDIENTS

- 2 tablespoons olive oil
- 1 cup chopped white onion
- 6 garlic cloves, crushed
- 1 medium New Mexico chile, stem and seeds removed
- 1 ½ cups unsalted vegetable broth
- 2 (20 ounce) cans green jackfruit in brine, rinsed and shredded
- 1 teaspoon chili powder
- ½ teaspoon kosher salt
- ½ teaspoon ground pepper
- 1 bay leaf
- 3 cups hot cooked brown rice
- 2 cups thinly sliced iceberg lettuce
- 1 ⅓ cups chopped plum tomatoes (about 3 medium)
- 1 cup unsalted canned black beans, rinsed
- ½ cup chopped fresh cilantro
- 1 lime, quartered

Nutritional Value: 340 calories | 21g protein. | 12g fat | 30g carbohydrate | Fiber: 23g

INGREDIENTS

1. Heat oil in a medium saucepan over medium-high heat. Add onion, garlic and chile; cook, stirring occasionally, until the onion is tender and browned, about 6 minutes.
2. Add broth; increase heat to high and bring to a boil. Partially cover and reduce heat to medium. Cook until the chile is tender, about 10 minutes. Transfer the mixture to a blender.
3. Remove center piece of blender lid (to allow steam to escape); secure the lid on the blender. Place a clean towel over the opening and process until very smooth, about 45 seconds. (Use caution when blending hot liquids.)
4. Return the chile sauce to the saucepan; add jackfruit, chili powder, salt, pepper and bay leaf. Bring to a simmer over medium-high heat. Reduce heat to medium-low, partially cover and cook until slightly thickened, 6 to 8 minutes. Discard the bay leaf.
5. Place 3/4 cup rice in each of 4 shallow bowls. Top each with 3/4 cup jackfruit mixture, 1/2 cup lettuce, 1/3 cup tomatoes, 1/4 cup beans and 2 tablespoons cilantro. Serve with lime wedges.

WHITE BEAN & SUN-DRIED TOMATO GNOCCHI

PREP TIME: 20 MINS **COOK TIME:** 40 MINS **SERVINGS:** 4

This White Bean & Sun-Dried Tomato Gnocchi is a delightful and nutritious dish, blending the flavors of sun-dried tomatoes with the wholesome goodness of white beans, creating a satisfying and fiber-rich meal.

INGREDIENTS

- ½ cup sliced oil-packed sun-dried tomatoes plus 2 tablespoons oil from the jar, divided
- 1 (16 ounce) package shelf-stable gnocchi
- 1 (15 ounce) can low-sodium cannellini beans, rinsed
- 1 (5 ounce) package baby spinach
- 1 large shallot, minced
- ⅓ cup low-sodium no-chicken broth or chicken broth
- ⅓ cup heavy cream
- 1 tablespoon lemon juice
- ¼ teaspoon salt
- ¼ teaspoon ground pepper
- 3 tablespoons fresh basil leaves

INGREDIENTS

1. Heat 1 tablespoon oil in a large nonstick skillet over medium-high heat. Add gnocchi and cook, stirring often, until plumped and starting to brown, about 5 minutes.
2. Add beans and spinach and cook until the spinach is wilted, about 1 minute. Transfer to a plate. bAdd the remaining 1 tablespoon oil to the pan and heat over medium heat. Add sun-dried tomatoes and shallot; cook, stirring, for 1 minute.
3. Increase heat to high and add broth. Cook until the liquid has mostly evaporated, about 2 minutes.
4. Reduce heat to medium and stir in cream, lemon juice, salt and pepper. Return the gnocchi mixture to the pan and stir to coat with the sauce. Serve topped with basil.

Nutritional Value: 341 calories | 21g protein. | 14g fat | 44g carbohydrate | Fiber: 26g

CREAMY SPINACH PASTA WITH WHITE BEANS

PREP TIME: 20 MINS   **COOK TIME:** 35 MINS   **SERVINGS:** 4

This Creamy Spinach Pasta with White Beans recipe is a delicious and nutritious way to enjoy a hearty, high-fiber meal. Packed with the goodness of spinach and white beans, this creamy pasta is not only satisfying but also easy to prepare. Perfect for a quick weeknight dinner or a wholesome lunch option. Let's get cooking!

INGREDIENTS

- 1 (5 ounce) package baby kale
- 1 (5 ounce) package baby spinach
- 8 ounces whole-wheat penne or rigatoni pasta
- 2 ounces cream cheese
- ½ cup shredded Gruyère cheese
- ½ cup torn fresh basil leaves, plus more for garnish
- 1 tablespoon lemon juice
- 1 clove garlic, grated
- ¾ teaspoon salt
- ½ teaspoon ground pepper
- 1 (15 ounce) can low-sodium white beans, rinsed

INGREDIENTS

1. Bring a large pot of water to a boil. Add the spinach and kale and cook until tender, about 3 minutes. With tongs or a slotted spoon, transfer the greens to a colander and rinse under cold water. Wrap in a clean towel and squeeze out as much liquid as possible. Keep the water boiling.
2. Add pasta to the boiling water and cook al dente according to package instructions.
3. Meanwhile, combine the greens, cream cheese, Gruyère, basil, lemon juice, garlic, salt and pepper in a food processor; process until the greens are finely chopped.
4. Reserve 1/4 cup of the pasta water; drain the cooked pasta and return to the pot. Add the reserved water to the food processor and process until the sauce is smooth.
5. Add beans and the sauce to the pasta and stir to combine. Top with more basil, if desired.

Nutritional Value: 350 calories | 22g protein. | 13g fat | 35g carbohydrate | Fiber: 25g

QUINOA, AVOCADO & CHICKPEA SALAD OVER MIXED GREENS

PREP TIME: 20 MINS **COOK TIME:** 40 MINS **SERVINGS:** 4

This wholesome salad combines the nutty flavors of quinoa with the creaminess of avocado and the hearty texture of chickpeas, served over a bed of fresh mixed greens. Packed with fiber and essential nutrients, this salad is not only delicious but also a great option for a healthy, fulfilling meal.

INGREDIENTS

- ⅔ cup water
- ⅓ cup quinoa
- ¼ teaspoon kosher salt or other coarse salt
- 1 clove garlic, crushed and peeled
- 2 teaspoons grated lemon zest
- 3 tablespoons lemon juice
- 3 tablespoons olive oil
- ¼ teaspoon ground pepper
- 1 cup rinsed no-salt-added canned chickpeas
- 1 medium carrot, shredded (1/2 cup)
- ½ avocado, diced
- 1 (5 ounce) package prewashed mixed greens, such as spring mix or baby kale-spinach blend (8 cups packed)

INGREDIENTS

1. Bring water to a boil in a small saucepan. Stir in quinoa. Reduce heat to low, cover, and simmer until all the liquid is absorbed, about 15 minutes. Use a fork to fluff and separate the grains; let cool for 5 minutes.
2. Meanwhile, sprinkle salt over garlic on a cutting board. Mash the garlic with the side of a spoon until a paste forms.
3. Scrape into a medium bowl. Whisk in lemon zest, lemon juice, oil, and pepper. Transfer 3 Tbsp. of the dressing to a small bowl and set aside.
4. Add chickpeas, carrot, and avocado to the bowl with the remaining dressing; gently toss to combine.
5. Let stand for 5 minutes to allow flavors to blend. Add the quinoa and gently toss to coat.
6. Place greens in a large bowl and toss with the reserved 3 Tbsp. dressing. Divide the greens between 2 plates and top with the quinoa mixture.

Nutritional Value: 333 calories | 26g protein. | 12g fat | 35g carbohydrate | Fiber: 25g

VEGAN CHICKPEA STEW

PREP TIME: 10 MINS **COOK TIME:** 45 MINS **SERVINGS:** 4

This hearty Chickpea Stew is not only delicious but also packed with fiber and plant-based goodness. It's a perfect meal for anyone looking to add more fiber to their diet.

INGREDIENTS

- 19 ounces canned chickpeas, do not drain
- 2 tablespoons olive oil
- 1 large onion, finely chopped
- 2 cloves garlic, grated
- 1 medium red bell pepper, diced
- 2 roma tomatoes, diced
- 2 medium carrots, peeled, diced
- 1 teaspoon dried parsley
- 1 teaspoon dried basil
- 1 teaspoon dried oregano
- 2 bay leaves
- 1/4 cup tomato paste
- 2 cups water
- 1 teaspoon salt
- ½ teaspoon ground black pepper

INGREDIENTS

1. In a large soup pot or dutch oven, saute the onions in the olive oil over medium heat. Cook for 4-5 minutes. Add the garlic and continue to cook for 1-2 minutes Add in the chickpeas (along with the liquid), bell pepper, tomatoes, and carrots.
2. Stir well and cook for 2-3 minutes. Add in the parsley, basil, oregano, bay leaves, black pepper, and tomato paste. Stir to combine. Add the water and stir. Cover and reduce heat to a simmer. Simmer for 30 minutes.
3. Check the seasoning and add the salt if needed. (Sometimes, the canned chickpeas will provide enough salt, but add more if you wish.)
With the lid off, allow to simmer for 5 minutes or so, or until desired consistency/thickness is achieved.

Nutritional Value: 280 calories | 26g protein. | 12g fat | 33g carbohydrate | Fiber: 23g

WHOLE WHEAT PASTA WITH TOMATO SAUCE AND VEGETABLES

PREP TIME: 20 MINS **COOK TIME:** 40 MINS **SERVINGS:** 4

This nutritious dish features whole wheat pasta in a savory tomato sauce, mixed with fresh vegetables. It's a healthy, satisfying meal that's quick and easy to prepare, perfect for a family dinner or hearty lunch.

INGREDIENTS

- 8 ounces whole wheat pasta such as penne
- 2 cups of warm prepared marinara sauce look for a low-fat, low-sugar variety
- 2 teaspoons olive oil
- 1 cup of small broccoli florets
- 1/2 cup of peeled carrots cut into 1/4 inch pieces
- 1 yellow squash halved and thinly sliced
- 1 cup of mushrooms thinly sliced
- 1/2 cup chopped onion
- 2 teaspoons minced garlic
- salt and pepper to taste
- 1/2 cup freshly grated parmesan cheese
- Optional: 2 tablespoons chopped parsley.

Nutritional Value: 377 calories | 21g protein. | 11g fat | 44g carbohydrate | Fiber: 26g

INGREDIENTS

1. Cook the pasta in salted water according to package instructions. While the pasta is cooking, heat the olive oil in a large pan over medium-high heat.
2. Add the onions to the pan and cook for 3-4 minutes, or until they've started to soften.
3. Add the broccoli, carrots, squash, and mushrooms to the pan. Season the vegetables with salt and pepper to taste.
4. Add 2 tablespoons of water to the pan. Cook for 5-7 minutes or until vegetables are tender and starting to brown.
5. Stir in the garlic and cook for 30 seconds more. Add the cooked pasta and marinara sauce in the pan; toss to coat.
6. Sprinkle with parmesan cheese and serve. Top with chopped parsley if desired.

LENTIL & SWEET POTATO SHEPHERD'S PIE

PREP TIME: 20 MINS   **COOK TIME:** 60 MINS   **SERVINGS:** 4

A colorful take on classic shepherd's pie with lentils, vegetables, and a fluffy sweet potato topping. You'll love this 10-ingredient plant-based meal!

INGREDIENTS

Sweet Potatoes:
- 3 large organic sweet potatoes (washed, peeled, and roughly chopped)
- 2 Tbsp coconut oil (or vegan butter, or sub vegetable broth)
- 1/4 tsp sea salt
- 1-2 Tbsp maple syrup (optional)

Filling:
- 1 Tbsp coconut or avocado oil (or sub water or vegetable broth)
- 1 medium onion (diced)
- 2 cloves garlic (minced)
- 1 1/2 cups uncooked brown or green lentils (rinsed and drained)
- 4 cups vegetable stock
- 2 tsp fresh thyme
- 1 bag (10 ounces) frozen mixed veggies: peas, carrots, green beans, and corn

Mushrooms (optional):
- 2 portobello mushrooms (sliced)
- 4 Tbsp balsamic vinegar
- 1 Tbsp melted coconut oil or avocado oil (or water if avoiding oil)
- Pinch of sea salt and black pepper
- 1 clove garlic (minced)

Nutritional Value: 273 calories | 26g protein. | 7g fat | 43g carbohydrate | Fiber: 25g

INGREDIENTS

1. Cook sweet potatoes until tender, drain, and mash. Add coconut oil, salt, pepper, and optional maple syrup. Set aside.
2. Preheat the oven to 425°F (220°C) and grease a 9x13-inch baking dish. If using mushrooms, marinate them in balsamic vinegar, oil (or water), salt, pepper, and garlic. Set aside.
3. In a pot, sauté onions and garlic until caramelized. Add salt, pepper, lentils, vegetable broth, and thyme. Simmer until lentils are tender. (Optional) Cook marinated mushrooms in a skillet.
4. In the last 10 minutes of lentil cooking, add frozen veggies. Drain excess vegetable stock, adjust seasoning, and transfer the lentil mixture to the baking dish. Top with (optional) mushrooms and mashed sweet potatoes. Bake for 20 minutes until lightly browned.
5. Let it cool briefly before serving. For storage, cool completely, cover, and refrigerate for up to 4-5 days or freeze for up to 1 month. Reheat in the microwave or oven. Enjoy!

GRILLED EGGPLANT SALAD WITH HALLOUMI & TOMATOES

PREP TIME: 20 MINS **COOK TIME:** 40 MINS **SERVINGS:** 2

Grilled Eggplant Salad with Halloumi & Tomatoes is a delightful Mediterranean-inspired dish that combines the smokiness of grilled eggplant with the creamy saltiness of halloumi cheese, topped off with the freshness of ripe tomatoes.

INGREDIENTS

- 2 medium sized eggplants or 4 Japanese eggplants
- 4 medium heirloom tomatoes (red and yellow)
- 8 oz haloumi cheese
- 1/3 C olive oil for brushing
- salt

Mint Dressing:

- 1/4 C mint leaves- packed
- 1/4 C Italian parsley- packed
- 1/4 C olive oil
- 1/8 C fresh lemon juice
- 1 T water 1 small garlic clove, minced
- 1/4 tsp salt cracked pepper
- Garnish with a few mint leaves

Nutritional Value: 344 calories | 23g protein. | 10g fat | 30g carbohydrate | Fiber: 23g

DIRECTIONS

1. Pre-heat grill, to med-high. Slice Eggplant to 1/3 inch thick pieces and brush with olive oil.
2. Slice halloumi into 1/2 inch thick pieces, brush with olive oil. Slice tomatoes into ½ inch slices, set aside.
3. Make dressing. Blend or process all ingredients in a blender or food processor… adding a little more water (only if necessary) to get the blender going. Do not blend it too smooth… you want to see pieces of the herbs.
4. Grill eggplant slices, closing lid, checking heat to make sure they don't burn, rotating as necessary. Eggplant is done when the white becomes slightly translucent. Stack them on a heat proof dish and cover tightly with foil so they continue cooking through.
5. You could place this on your upper grill rack if you have one, or just set aside, covered.
6. Grill the Halloumi cheese just until grill marks appear. Arrange eggplant, tomatoes and cheese all on a platter, layering. Drizzle liberally with the dressing and a sprinkle of salt and pepper, and garnish with fresh mint leaves. Serve at room temp.
7. If you want to serve this Napoleon Style- a stacked individual portion, layer eggplant, tomato, and haloumi spooning a little mint dressing on each layer, until 4-5 inches tall. Skewer with a skewer or sturdy rosemary sprig (removing bottom rosemary leaves).

FETA AND WATERMELON GRAIN BOWLS

PREP TIME: 20 MINS   **COOK TIME:** 45 MINS   **SERVINGS:** 2

These Feta and Watermelon Grain Bowls are a refreshing and satisfying blend of salty feta, sweet watermelon, and wholesome grains. Packed with fiber and flavor, this dish makes for a delightful and nutritious meal.

INGREDIENTS

- 1 ½ cups semi-pearled farro
- 3 tablespoons olive oil
- 2 tablespoons fresh lime juice (from 1 lime)
- 1 ¾ teaspoons kosher salt
- ½ teaspoon freshly ground black pepper
- 3 cups cubed seedless watermelon (1 lb.)
- 1 avocado, cubed
- 4 ounces feta cheese, cut into 8 slabs
- ½ cup packed fresh cilantro leaves
- ¼ cup unsalted roasted pumpkin seeds (pepitas)

DIRECTIONS

1. Bring a large saucepan of water to a boil over high. Add farro and cook, stirring occasionally, until just tender, about 20 minutes. Drain and spread on a large baking sheet. Let cool for about 10 minutes.
2. Whisk oil, lime juice, salt, and pepper in a small bowl. Toss watermelon and farro in a large bowl. Drizzle with most of lime juice mixture and gently toss to coat.
3. Top with avocado and feta, drizzle with remaining dressing, and sprinkle with cilantro and pepitas.

Nutritional Value: 351 calories | 25g protein. | 27g fat | 34g carbohydrate | Fiber: 25g

ROASTED ROOT VEGGIE QUINOA BOWLS

PREP TIME: 20 MINS　　**COOK TIME:** 30 MINS　　**SERVINGS:** 4

Roasted Root Veggie Quinoa Bowls are a wholesome and satisfying meal option, packed with fiber and flavor. This recipe combines the earthy goodness of roasted root vegetables with protein-rich quinoa to create a hearty and nutritious dish. It's not only delicious but also easy to prepare, making it a perfect choice for a healthy meal.

INGREDIENTS

- 1 10-oz. pkg. fresh butternut squash, cut into 3/4-in. cubes
- 4 parsnips, peeled and cut into 3/4 in. cubes (about 2 cups)
- 8 oz. Brussels sprouts, trimmed and quartered lengthwise
- 1 small red onion
- 1/4 cup plus 2 Tbsp. olive oil, divided
- 2 tsp. kosher salt, divided
- 1 cup quinoa
- 3 cups fresh baby spinach
- 1 Tbsp. white balsamic or apple cider vinegar
- 1 tsp. Dijon mustard
- 1/2 cup hummus

DIRECTIONS

1. Place a large rimmed baking sheet in oven and preheat oven to 450°F. Toss together squash, parsnips, Brussels sprouts, onion, 2 tablespoons oil, and 1 1/2 teaspoons salt in a large bowl.
2. Carefully spread vegetable mixture on preheated baking sheet. Return to oven and roast, tossing halfway through, until tender and browned, about 20 minutes. Let cool on baking sheet for 5 minutes.
3. Meanwhile, cook quinoa according to package directions. Transfer to a large bowl.
4. Add spinach and remaining 1/2 teaspoon salt. Toss until spinach is slightly wilted.
5. Whisk vinegar and mustard in a small bowl. Gradually drizzle in remaining 1/4 cup oil, whisking constantly. Stir 2 tablespoons vinaigrette into quinoa.
6. Divide quinoa among 4 bowls. Top with roasted vegetables. Dollop with hummus and drizzle with remaining vinaigrette. Serve warm or at room temperature.

Nutritional Value: 332 calories | 26g protein. | 12g fat | 34g carbohydrate | Fiber: 25g

RICE BOWL WITH CHIPOTLE BLACK BEANS

PREP TIME: 15 MINS   **COOK TIME:** 30 MINS   **SERVINGS:** 4

Quinoa and Black Bean Stuffed Peppers are a delicious and nutritious dish packed with fiber, thanks to the combination of quinoa and black beans. These stuffed peppers make for a wholesome and satisfying meal.

INGREDIENTS

- 2 tablespoons extra-virgin olive oil
- 2 cups sliced red onion
- 4 cups cooked white rice
- 1 (15-oz.) can black beans
- 1 tablespoon chopped canned chipotle peppers in adobo sauce
- ¾ teaspoon kosher salt
- 2 cups halved cherry tomatoes
- ¼ cup fresh cilantro leaves
- ¼ cup sour cream
- lime wedges, for serving

DIRECTIONS

1. Heat the oil in a large nonstick skillet over medium-high. Add the onion; cook, stirring occasionally, until browned, 5 minutes.
2. Add the rice; cook, stirring occasionally, 2 minutes. Divide the rice mixture among 4 bowls.
3. Drain and rinse the beans, reserving 3 tablespoons of their liquid. Add the beans, reserved liquid, chipotles, and salt to the skillet. Cook over medium-high, stirring occasionally, until warmed through, about 2 minutes.
4. Divide the bean mixture and tomatoes among 4 bowls. Top evenly with the cilantro and sour cream. Serve with lime wedges.

Nutritional Value: 344 calories | 26g protein. | 11g fat | 35g carbohydrate | Fiber: 25g

GREEN SALAD

PREP TIME: 15 MINS   **COOK TIME:** 30 MINS   **SERVINGS:** 4

This gorgeous salad combines fresh shrimp, cucumber, artichoke hearts and cherry tomatoes with homemade green goddess dressing. The dressing is beautifully green and creamy with avocado (loaded with good-for-you fiber) and fresh herbs. Buttermilk and a dash of rice vinegar add tang.

INGREDIENTS

- ½ avocado, peeled and pitted
- ¾ cup nonfat buttermilk
- 2 tablespoons chopped fresh herbs, such as tarragon, sorrel and/or chives
- 2 teaspoons tarragon vinegar, or white-wine vinegar
- 1 teaspoon anchovy paste, or minced anchovy fillet
- 8 cups bite-size pieces green leaf lettuce
- 12 ounces peeled and deveined cooked shrimp, (21-25 per pound; see Ingredient note)
- ½ cucumber, sliced
- 1 cup cherry or grape tomatoes
- 1 cup canned chickpeas, rinsed
- 1 cup rinsed and chopped canned artichoke hearts
- ½ cup chopped celery

Nutritional Value: 262 calories | 22g protein. | 8g fat | 31g carbohydrate | Fiber: 25g

DIRECTIONS

1. Puree avocado, buttermilk, herbs, vinegar and anchovy in a blender until smooth.
2. Divide lettuce among 4 plates. Top with shrimp, cucumber, tomatoes, chickpeas, artichoke hearts and celery.
3. Drizzle the dressing over the salads.

ROASTED VEGETABLE BOWLS WITH PESTO

PREP TIME: 15 MINS   **COOK TIME:** 20 MINS   **SERVINGS:** 4

Enjoy a wholesome and delicious meal with these Roasted Vegetable Bowls with Pesto. Packed with fiber and flavor, this recipe is sure to satisfy your taste buds and keep you feeling full and energized.

INGREDIENTS

- 3 tablespoons extra-virgin olive oil, divided
- ½ teaspoon garlic powder
- ¼ teaspoon salt
- ¼ teaspoon ground pepper
- 4 cups broccoli florets
- 2 medium red bell peppers, quartered
- 1 cup sliced red onion
- 3 cups cooked brown rice
- 1 (15 ounce) can chickpeas, rinsed
- 4 tablespoons prepared pesto

DIRECTIONS

1. Preheat oven to 450 degrees F. Whisk 2 tablespoons oil, garlic powder, salt and pepper together in a large bowl. Add broccoli, peppers and onion; toss to coat.
2. Transfer to a large rimmed baking sheet and roast, stirring once, until the vegetables are tender, about 20 minutes. Chop the peppers when cool enough to handle.
3. Stir the remaining 1 tablespoon oil into rice. Place about 3/4 cup of the rice in each of four 2-cup microwave-safe, lidded containers.
4. Divide chickpeas and the roasted vegetables among the bowls. Top each with 1 tablespoon pesto.
5. To reheat: Microwave each container on High until heated through, 1 to 2 minutes.

Nutritional Value: 384 calories | 21g protein. | 21g fat | 30g carbohydrate | Fiber: 25g

BLACK BEAN & SLAW BAGEL

PREP TIME: 10 MINS   **COOK TIME:** 20 MINS   **SERVINGS:** 2

This easy open-face sandwich recipe uses a jalapeño-Cheddar bagel, but a plain bagel would work just as well. Top each bagel half with black beans and fresh slaw for a satisfying bite.

INGREDIENTS

- 2 cups shredded green cabbage
- 2 tablespoons chopped fresh cilantro
- 2 tablespoons lime juice
- ⅛ teaspoon salt
- ½ avocado, mashed
- 1 jalapeño-Cheddar bagel, halved and toasted
- 1 cup rinsed no-salt-added canned black beans, heated

DIRECTIONS

1. Toss cabbage, cilantro, lime juice and salt in a medium bowl.
2. Spread avocado on the top of each bagel half. Top each with 1/2 cup beans and half the slaw.

Nutritional Value: 223 calories | 21g protein. | 10g fat | 34g carbohydrate | Fiber: 26g

CHOPPED SALAD WITH SRIRACHA TOFU & PEANUT DRESSING

PREP TIME: 10 MINS   **COOK TIME:** 20 MINS   **SERVINGS:** 4

This Chopped Salad with Sriracha Tofu & Peanut Dressing is a flavorful and nutritious dish that's packed with fiber and protein. The combination of crispy tofu, fresh vegetables, and a zesty peanut dressing creates a satisfying and healthy meal.

INGREDIENTS

- 1 (10 ounce) package kale, Brussels sprout, broccoli and cabbage salad mix
- 1 (12 ounce) package frozen shelled edamame, thawed
- 2 (7 ounce) packages Sriracha-flavored baked tofu, cubed
- 1/2 cup spicy peanut vinaigrette

DIRECTIONS

1. Divide salad mix among 4 single-serving containers with lids. Top each with 1/2 cup edamame and one-fourth of the tofu.
2. Transfer 2 tablespoons vinaigrette into each of 4 small lidded containers and refrigerate for up to 4 days.
3. Seal the salad containers and refrigerate for up to 4 days. Dress with vinaigrette up to 1 day before serving.

Nutritional Value: 322 calories | 27g protein. | 15g fat | 44g carbohydrate | Fiber: 25g

CHIPOTLE TOFU CHILAQUILES

PREP TIME: 20 MINS   **COOK TIME:** 30 MINS   **SERVINGS:** 2

Get ready to tantalize your taste buds with this delicious and nutritious Chipotle Tofu Chilaquiles recipe. Packed with protein and fiber, it's a fantastic way to start your day or enjoy a hearty meal any time. The smoky chipotle flavor combined with crispy tofu and tortilla chips will leave you craving more!

INGREDIENTS

FOR THE CHILAQUILES:
- 5 small yellow corn tortillas
- 1/2 large white onion (diced)
  2 cloves garlic (minced)
- 1 15-ounce can crushed tomatoes or tomato sauce
- 1 chipotle pepper in adobo sauce (canned)
- 1 Tbsp adobo sauce (add more or less depending on preferred spice)
- 1/2 cup veggie stock

For The Tofu:
- 8 ounces extra-firm tofu (drained and pressed in a clean towel for 15 minutes
- 1/2 tsp ground cumin
- 1/2 tsp garlic powder
- 1/4 tsp chili powder
- 1/4 tsp sea salt
- Toppings (optional)
- Vegan Mexican Cheese
- Diced onion and/or fresh cilantro
  Salsa or hot sauce
- Lime juice

Nutritional Value: 351 calories | 26g protein. | 15g fat | 32g carbohydrate | Fiber: 25g

DIRECTIONS

1. Start by quickly pressing/draining your tofu in a clean kitchen towel with a heavy pot on top, and preheating oven to 350 degrees F (176 C).
2. IF BAKING YOUR OWN TORTILLAS: Lightly brush or spray both sides of your tortillas with olive or avocado oil and lightly dust them with sea salt. Stack and cut into triangles and arrange in a single layer on a large baking sheet.
3. Bake for 10-12 minutes, flipping once halfway through, until crisp and just slightly golden brown. Set aside. If using regular chips, skip this step. While chips are baking, heat a large skillet over medium heat and prep onion and garlic.
4. Once hot, add 1 Tbsp olive or avocado oil and onion. Cook, stirring frequently, until soft and slightly browned – 3 minutes. Then add garlic and cook for 1-2 minutes more.
5. Add tomato sauce, diced chipotle and adobo sauce, and veggie stock. Heat until bubbly. Then reduce heat to low and simmer for 5 minutes.
6. Transfer sauce to a blender (optional). For a completely smooth sauce, blend well. For a chunkier sauce, pulse and leave some texture. Set aside.
7. Use a fork to crumble the tofu and place skillet back over medium heat (no need to rinse or wipe clean – the remaining sauce adds more flavor).
8. Add a bit of oil to the pan and then add tofu. Let lightly brown for 3-4 minutes, stirring once or twice. Then add seasonings (chili powder, salt, garlic powder and cumin) and stir. Cook for another 2 minutes, then remove from pan and set aside.
9. Add chips to the pan and pour over sauce, stirring quickly to coat. Then top with tofu scramble, fresh onion, and cilantro and serve immediately.
10. Additional toppings might include hot sauce, lime juice, salsa and/or Vegan Mexican Cheese. Serves 2-3 as original recipe is written. Best when fresh.

ROASTED SWEET POTATO & KALE HASH

PREP TIME: 10 MINS **COOK TIME:** 35 MINS **SERVINGS:** 2

This dish is a perfect balance of savory and sweet, offering a hearty and healthy meal that's quick and easy to prepare. Packed with the goodness of sweet potatoes, kale, and a touch of spice, it's a satisfying way to boost your fiber intake while tantalizing your taste buds."

INGREDIENTS

Scramble
- 8 ounces extra-firm tofu (organic when possible)
- 2 small sweet potatoes
- 2 Tbsp melted coconut oil (divided)
- 3 1/4 tsp tandoori masala spice (divided)
- 1 tsp coconut sugar
- 1/2 tsp each sea salt + black pepper (divided)
- 1 red onion
- 2 Tbsp fresh parsley (plus more for serving)
- 1/8 tsp ground turmeric
- 1 large bundle kale

For Serving Optional
- Hummus (store bought or this recipe)
- Hot sauce (tapatio is my favorite!)

Nutritional Value: 322 calories | 24g protein. | 10g fat | 35g carbohydrate | Fiber: 25g

DIRECTIONS

1. Preheat your oven to 400 degrees F (204°C). Wrap the tofu in a clean towel and place something heavy on top, like a cast-iron skillet, to press out excess moisture.
2. While the tofu is pressing, season the sweet potatoes. Toss them with 1/2 tablespoon of oil, 1 teaspoon of tandoori masala spice, coconut sugar, and a pinch of salt and pepper. Make sure the seasonings coat the sweet potatoes evenly.
3. Season the onion by tossing it with 1/2 tablespoon of oil, 1/4 teaspoon of tandoori spice, and a pinch of salt and pepper. Ensure the seasonings coat the onions thoroughly.
4. Place the seasoned onions and sweet potatoes in the preheated oven. Roast them for 25-35 minutes, flipping once halfway through. They should be done when the onions are brown and caramelized, and the sweet potatoes are fork-tender.
5. Remove them from the oven and set aside.
   While the vegetables are roasting, crumble the pressed tofu into small pieces using two forks. Season the crumbled tofu with fresh parsley, turmeric, and a pinch of salt and pepper. Set the tofu aside.
6. Heat a large skillet over medium-high heat. Add 1/2 tablespoon of oil, the crumbled tofu, and 1 teaspoon of tandoori masala spice. Sauté for about 5 minutes, stirring occasionally, to dry and brown the tofu. Once done, remove the tofu from the skillet and set it aside.
7. In the same skillet, add the remaining 1/2 tablespoon of oil and kale. Season thekale with a pinch of salt, pepper, and 1 teaspoon of tandoori masala spice. Sauté the kale, stirring frequently, until it wilts and browns, which should take about 3-4 minutes.
8. Push the wilted kale to one side of the pan and return the sautéed tofu to the skillet to warm it. Turn off the heat, but keep the skillet on the burner.
   To serve, divide the sautéed kale among 2 (or 3, based on your preference) serving plates. Top with the roasted sweet potatoes and onions, and then the sautéed tofu.
9. Sprinkle with the remaining chopped parsley, and feel free to add hot sauce for extra flavor or serve with a generous spoonful of hummus if desired.
10. This dish is best enjoyed fresh, but leftovers can be covered and stored in the refrigerator for 2-3 days. To reheat, use a microwave or place it on a baking sheet in a 350-degree F (174°C) oven for 15-20 minutes, or until warmed through.

CHEESY BROCCOLI HASHBROWN BAKE

PREP TIME: 20 MINS   **COOK TIME:** 40 MINS   **SERVINGS:** 4

Indulge in the delightful flavors of our Cheesy Broccoli Hashbrown Bake, a comforting and wholesome casserole that's perfect for breakfast, brunch, or as a side dish. This easy-to-make recipe combines crispy hash browns, tender broccoli, and a creamy, cheesy blend for a mouthwatering dish that will leave your taste buds singing. Whether you're serving a crowd or enjoying a cozy family meal, this bake is sure to become a favorite in your kitchen.

INGREDIENTS

Sauce Ingredients:
- 1/2 cup raw cashews (or sunflower seeds for a nut-free option)
- 1/2 cup sliced carrots (substitute red or orange bell pepper if desired)
- 5-6 cloves of garlic
- 5-6 tablespoons nutritional yeast
- 3/4 teaspoon sea salt, plus more for taste
- 1 1/4 cups unsweetened plain dairy-free milk (e.g., almond, rice, or oat milk)

Vegetables Ingredients:
- 5 cups packed shredded golden potatoes (or frozen hash browns, with extra moisture squeezed out)
- 5 cups chopped broccoli (bite-sized pieces)
- 3/4 teaspoon sea salt
- 3/4 teaspoon black pepper, plus more for taste
- 1 teaspoon garlic powder
- 4 tablespoons nutritional yeast

Nutritional Value: 333 calories | 21g protein. | 15g fat | 30g carbohydrate | Fiber: 26g

DIRECTIONS

1. Preheat your oven to 400°F (204°C) and lightly grease a 9x13-inch (or similar-sized) baking dish (adjust the pan size if you're altering the batch size).
2. In a bowl, soak the cashews and carrots in very hot water for 20 minutes. Then, drain the water and transfer them to a high-speed blender.
3. Grate the potatoes using a box grater with medium-sized holes or use a food processor to cut them into small pieces and grate. Place the grated potatoes in a thin dish towel or nut milk bag and squeeze out the extra liquid to prevent a soggy hashbrown bake.
4. Add the grated, drained potatoes and chopped broccoli to the prepared baking dish. Sprinkle with sea salt, black pepper, garlic powder, and nutritional yeast, then toss to combine.
5. In the blender with cashews and carrots, add garlic, nutritional yeast, sea salt, and almond milk. Blend until smooth and creamy. Adjust the flavor to your liking, adding more garlic for extra zest, nutritional yeast for a cheesier flavor, and salt for added saltiness. It should have a robust garlic, cheesy, and salty taste.
6. Pour the sauce over the potatoes and broccoli and toss to combine. Smooth the top using the back of a spoon. Bake for 35-40 minutes, or until it's golden brown with slightly crispy edges.
7. For even crispier edges, you can turn on the broiler in the last few minutes. Enjoy this dish best when it's fresh.
8. Store any leftovers covered in the refrigerator for up to 3-4 days. Note that it's not suitable for freezing. Reheat in a 350°F (176°C) oven until warmed through.

CURRIED QUINOA CHICKPEA BURGERS

PREP TIME: 10 MINS

COOK TIME: 60 MINS

SERVINGS: 4

Indulge in the delectable world of Curried Quinoa Chickpea Burgers - a healthy and flavorful twist on traditional burgers. These patties are a culinary delight, combining quinoa, chickpeas, and a medley of aromatic spices. In just a few easy steps, you can whip up a burger that's not only delicious but also loaded with fiber, making it a guilt-free treat for any time of day.

INGREDIENTS

For the Quinoa:
- 1 cup cooked and cooled quinoa
  For the Chickpeas:
- 1 15-oz can chickpeas, rinsed, drained, and dried
- 1 Tbsp avocado or coconut oil (optional)
- Pinch of sea salt
- 1 tsp Curry Powder (or store-bought)

For the Potatoes:
- 1 1/2 cups small diced, peeled yellow potatoes
- 1 Tbsp avocado or coconut oil
  Pinch of sea salt
- 1 tsp Curry Powder (or store-bought)
  3-4 Tbsp water

For the Rest:
- 2/3 cup raw or roasted cashews (substitute seeds if nut-sensitive)
- 1 small serrano pepper, deseeded and minced (optional)
- 2 Tbsp fresh minced ginger (skin removed)
- 4 cloves garlic, minced
- 3/4 tsp sea salt (divided)
- 2 Tbsp harissa paste (substitute tomato paste for less heat, or a curry paste of your choice)
- 1/2 cup chopped fresh cilantro (optional)

For Serving (optional):
- Butter Lettuce Leaves or Mixed Greens
- Sliced Red Onion
- Spicy Mango Chutney
- Vegan Naan

DIRECTIONS

1. If you haven't prepared your quinoa yet, cook and cool it completely before using. Preheat your oven to 375 degrees F (190 C).
2. On a parchment-lined baking sheet, toss the rinsed and dried chickpeas with oil (if using), salt, and curry powder. Bake for 20 minutes or until the chickpeas appear cracked and feel dry to the touch. Remove them from the oven and set aside. Keep the oven on.
3. In the meantime, add the diced potatoes (cut into bite-sized pieces) to an oven-safe skillet along with oil, salt, and curry powder. Cover and cook for 4 minutes. Then decrease the heat to medium-low, add water, and cover again. Continue cooking the potatoes until they are browned on the edges and tender. Turn off the heat and use a fork or potato masher to mash them until nearly creamy with few chunks. Set aside.
4. In a food processor, combine the cooked chickpeas, cashews, serrano pepper (optional), ginger, garlic, salt, curry powder, harissa paste, and cilantro (optional). Blend into a semi-loose dough. Then add the cooked and cooled quinoa and pulse to combine until a textured dough forms (you're not looking for a purée).
5. Transfer the mixture to a mixing bowl and add the mashed potatoes. Stir tocombine (avoid adding the potatoes to the food processor to prevent gumminess when overmixed). Taste and adjust the flavor as needed, adding more curry powder for intense curry flavor, salt for saltiness, or harissa paste for more spice.
6. Divide the mixture into roughly 2/3-cup portions and form them into 3/4-inch thick discs.
   Heat the same oven-safe skillet over medium heat. Once hot, add a little oil and the burger patties. Cook for 2-3 minutes or until the bottom side is golden brown. Flip the patties and then transfer the pan to the oven to bake for 12-15 minutes (optional but ensures the center is fully cooked).
7. For serving, enjoy the patties in a traditional bun, with naan, on a salad, or wrapped in a butter lettuce leaf. Add sliced red onions and mango chutney (optional).
8. Store leftover patties covered in the refrigerator for up to 3-4 days. If you want to freeze them, either freeze them once cooked and cooled or before sautéing and baking. Add patties to a freezer-safe container and freeze for up to 1 month. Reheat in a 375-degree F (190 C) oven until warmed through.

Nutritional Value: 254calories | 21g protein | 15g fat | 30g carbohydrate | Fiber: 24g

GRILLED ROMAINE CAESAR SALAD WITH HERBED WHITE BEANS

PREP TIME: 20 MINS
COOK TIME: 30 MINS
SERVINGS: 4

Elevate your salad game with our Grilled Romaine Caesar Salad featuring flavorful herbed white beans. This high-fiber, plant-based dish combines the smoky goodness of grilled romaine lettuce with a creamy Caesar dressing and zesty white beans, making it a healthy and delectable choice for your next meal.

INGREDIENTS

Salad:
- 2 large heads of romaine lettuce
- 1 tablespoon avocado oil or olive oil (avocado oil is preferable for grilling)
- A pinch of sea salt and black pepper
- Vegan parmesan cheese for topping (optional)

Beans:
- 1 (15-ounce) can of white or butter beans, rinsed and drained
- 1 clove of minced garlic
- 1 tablespoon lemon juice
- 1 tablespoon olive oil or avocado oil
- 1/4 teaspoon each of sea salt and black pepper
- 2 tablespoons fresh parsley, chopped (plus more for topping)

Dressing:
- 1 cup raw cashews
- 1 teaspoon dijon mustard
- 1/2 teaspoon each of sea salt and black pepper (plus more to taste)
- 8-12 medium cloves of fresh garlic, chopped
- 4 teaspoons capers in brine
- 2 teaspoons brine juice from capers
- 6 tablespoons lemon juice (2 large lemons yield ~6 tablespoons or 90 ml)
- 3-4 tablespoons olive oil
- 1 teaspoon chickpea (or soy) miso paste (optional)
- 1 teaspoon pure maple syrup (or sub stevia to taste)
- 1/2 cup hot water (plus more to thin)

DIRECTIONS

1. If using a grill, preheat it. If not, use a grill pan. Prepare the romaine by leaving it whole but removing any bruised or broken leaves.
2. Rinse the heads of lettuce to remove any dirt and pat them dry with a clean towel. Carefully cut the romaine heads in half lengthwise, then use a paper or cloth towel to clean any remaining bits of dirt from the inner leaves.
3. Arrange the halves on a baking sheet and lightly drizzle the cut sides with oil. Sprinkle with salt and pepper and set aside.
4. In a small mixing bowl, combine the rinsed and drained white beans with garlic, lemon juice, olive oil, sea salt, black pepper, and fresh parsley. Toss to combine and adjust the flavor as needed by adding more lemon, salt, or garlic. Set aside.
5. Prepare the dressing by adding raw cashews, dijon mustard, salt, pepper, fresh garlic, capers, brine juice, lemon juice, olive oil, miso paste (if using), maple syrup, and hot water to a small or high-speed blender.
6. Blend until the mixture is creamy and smooth, scraping down the sides as needed. Add enough water to thin it to a pourable consistency. Adjust the flavor by adding more lemon, salt, maple syrup, or garlic. Set aside.
7. If using a grill pan, heat it over high heat and lightly coat the surface with oil. Place the romaine halves on the hot grill or grill pan and grill for 1-2 minutes on each side until grill marks are visible. Be careful when turning, as romaine can become fragile when exposed to heat.
8. Remove the grilled romaine and transfer it to a large cutting board. Top it with the white beans and your desired amount of dressing. You can garnish with vegan parmesan cheese and extra parsley if you like (optional).
9. We recommend chopping the salad into large bites with a knife on the cutting board, lightly tossing it, and transferring it to a serving bowl or platter. This salad is best when served fresh.
10. Any leftover dressing can be stored in the refrigerator for 5-7 days.

Nutritional Value: 354 calories | 21g protein. | 15g fat | 35g carbohydrate | Fiber: 25g

ROASTED PLANTAIN & BLACK BEAN VEGAN BOWL

PREP TIME: 10 MINS   **COOK TIME:** 40 MINS   **SERVINGS:** 2

Indulge in the delectable world of Curried Quinoa Chickpea Burgers - a healthy and flavorful twist on traditional burgers. These patties are a culinary delight, combining quinoa, chickpeas, and a medley of aromatic spices. In just a few easy steps, you can whip up a burger that's not only delicious but also loaded with fiber, making it a guilt-free treat for any time of day.

INGREDIENTS

For Roasted Plantains:
- 4 large ripe plantains (yellow with brown spots), peeled and cut into 1/2-inch rounds
- 1.5 tablespoons of coconut oil (or substitute with maple syrup or water if avoiding oil)
- A pinch of sea salt

For Rice + Beans:
- 4 cups of cooked brown or white rice (or substitute with cauliflower rice for a grain-free option)
- 2 15-ounce cans of black beans (slightly drained)
- Sea salt to taste
- Ground cumin and chili powder (optional)

For Slaw:
- 3 cups of finely shredded green or purple cabbage
- 1 cup of finely chopped green onions

Optional Toppings:
- Guacamole or ripe avocado
- Fresh chopped cilantro
- Lime wedges
- Chimichurri
- Salsa
- Roasted Beet Relish
- Habanero Hot Sauce

Nutritional Value: 344 calories | 26g protein. | 7g fat | 45g carbohydrate | Fiber: 27g

DIRECTIONS

1. Preheat your oven to 425 degrees F (218 C) and line a baking sheet with parchment paper. Arrange the plantain rounds on the prepared baking sheet.
2. Prepare the brown or white rice according to the package instructions. See notes for alternative cooking methods. Warm the black beans in a small saucepan on the stovetop, adding salt to taste. Optionally, season with ground cumin and chili powder to taste. Heat over medium heat and then simmer to keep warm.
3. Toss the plantains with coconut oil (or maple syrup/water) and a pinch of salt, ensuring they're evenly coated. Bake in the preheated oven for approximately 15 minutes or until they turn golden brown and slightly caramelized. Set aside.
4. Create the slaw by combining the shredded cabbage and chopped green onions in a mixing bowl. For a more flavorful slaw, see the notes for additional options. Prepare any other desired toppings at this time, such as sauces, avocado or guacamole, and fresh cilantro.
5. To serve, assemble your bowls by layering rice, black beans, roasted plantains, vegetable slaw, and any other desired toppings or sauces.
6. Popular choices include habanero hot sauce, lime wedges, avocado, and cilantro.
7. This dish is best enjoyed when freshly assembled, although any leftovers can be stored separately in the refrigerator for up to 4 days.

VEGGIE NIÇOISE SALAD WITH RED CURRY GREEN BEANS

PREP TIME: 20 MINS   **COOK TIME:** 50 MINS   **SERVINGS:** 4

Indulge in a burst of Mediterranean flavors with our Veggie Niçoise Salad, elevated with the exotic twist of Red Curry Green Beans. This vibrant and nutritious salad is a delightful fusion of crispy green beans roasted with red curry paste, mixed with a medley of fresh vegetables, and topped with perfectly cooked eggs.

INGREDIENTS

DRESSING
- 1 large shallot, minced
- 1 garlic clove, minced
- 1 tablespoon Dijon mustard
- 3 tablespoons white wine vinegar
- ½ cup extra-virgin olive oil
- Kosher salt
- Freshly ground black pepper

SALAD
- ¾ pound new potatoes
- 2 tablespoons white wine vinegar
- 2 tablespoons extra-virgin olive oil
- ½ tablespoon red curry paste
- ½ pound green beans, trimmed
- Kosher salt
- Freshly ground black pepper
- 4 cups baby arugula
- 1 bunch radishes, quartered
- ½ English cucumber, thinly sliced
- 3 large hard-boiled eggs, halved lengthwise
- 1 cup halved Niçoise olives

Nutritional Value: 256 calories | 25g protein. | 20g fat | 40g carbohydrate | Fiber: 25g

DIRECTIONS

1. MAKE THE DRESSING: In a small bowl, whisk together the shallots, garlic, mustard and vinegar. Gradually whisk in the oil until the mixture is thick. Season with salt and pepper.
2. MAKE THE SALAD: In a large pot, cover the potatoes with 1 inch of water and bring to a boil. Cook until the potatoes are fork-tender, 8 to 10 minutes. Drain and cool slightly.
3. Meanwhile, in a medium bowl, whisk together the vinegar, olive oil and curry paste. Add the green beans and toss well to coat. Season with salt and pepper.
4. In a large bowl, toss the arugula with half of the dressing and then transfer to a large platter. In three separate small bowls, toss the potatoes, radishes and cucumber slices with the remaining dressing.
5. Top the arugula with the potatoes, green beans, radishes, cucumber, hard-boiled eggs and olives.

CHICKPEA AND VEGETABLE COCONUT CURRY

PREP TIME: 10 MINS   **COOK TIME:** 30 MINS   **SERVINGS:** 4

This quick and easy recipe combines the rich creaminess of coconut milk with the earthy goodness of chickpeas and a medley of vibrant vegetables. It's a satisfying, plant-based meal that's bursting with flavor and nutrition.

INGREDIENTS

- 1 tablespoon extra-virgin olive oil
- 1 red onion, thinly sliced
- 1 red bell pepper, thinly sliced
- 1 tablespoon fresh ginger, minced
- 3 garlic cloves, minced
- 1 small head cauliflower, cut into bite-size florets
- 2 teaspoons chili powder
- 1 teaspoon ground coriander
- 3 tablespoons red curry paste
- One 14-ounce can coconut milk
- 1 lime, halved
- One 28-ounce can chickpeas
- 1½ cups frozen peas
- Kosher salt and freshly ground black pepper
- Steamed rice, for serving (optional)
- ¼ cup chopped fresh cilantro
- 4 scallions, thinly sliced

DIRECTIONS

1. In a large saucepan, heat the olive oil over medium heat. Add the onion and bell pepper, and sauté until nearly tender, about 5 minutes. Add the ginger and garlic, and sauté until fragrant, about 1 minute.
2. Add the cauliflower and toss well to combine. Stir in the chili powder, coriander and red curry paste, and cook until the mixture begins to caramelize, about 1 minute.
3. Stir in the coconut milk and bring the mixture to a simmer over medium-low heat. Cover the saucepan and continue to simmer until the cauliflower is tender, 8 to 10 minutes.
4. Remove the lid and squeeze lime juice into the curry, stirring well to combine. Add the chickpeas and peas, season with salt and pepper, and bring the mixture back to a simmer.
5. Serve with rice, if desired. Garnish each portion with 1 tablespoon cilantro and 1 tablespoon scallions.

Nutritional Value: 350 calories | 26g protein. | 12g fat | 34g carbohydrate | Fiber: 32g

SALMON BOWL WITH FARRO, BLACK BEANS AND TAHINI DRESSING

PREP TIME: 10 MINS   **COOK TIME:** 40 MINS   **SERVINGS:** 1

Indulge in a burst of Mediterranean flavors with our Veggie Niçoise Salad, elevated with the exotic twist of Red Curry Green Beans. This vibrant and nutritious salad is a delightful fusion of crispy green beans roasted with red curry paste, mixed with a medley of fresh vegetables, and topped with perfectly cooked eggs.

INGREDIENTS

- 2 tablespoons tahini
- Zest and juice of 1 lemon
- ½ teaspoon turmeric, divided
- ¼ teaspoon garlic powder
- 6 tablespoons extra-virgin olive oil, divided
- Kosher salt and freshly ground black pepper
- ¼ cup farro
- ½ cup cooked black beans
- ½ teaspoon cumin
- 6 ounces salmon
- 1½ teaspoons smoked paprika
- ½ teaspoon coriander
- 4 Boston lettuce leaves
- ½ avocado, thinly sliced
- 2 scallions, thinly sliced
- ¼ Fresno chile, thinly sliced

DIRECTIONS

1. In a small bowl, whisk together the tahini, lemon zest, lemon juice, ¼ teaspoon of the turmeric and the garlic powder. Gradually add 3 tablespoons of the olive oil and whisk until the dressing is thick and well emulsified. Season with salt and pepper.
2. Bring the farro and 1 cup water to a simmer in a small pot over medium heat. Reduce the heat to low and simmer until the farro is very tender, 20 to 25 minutes. Set aside.
3. Combine the beans, 1 tablespoon of the olive oil and the cumin in a small bowl. Set aside.
4. Season the salmon with the smoked paprika, coriander, remaining ¼ teaspoon turmeric, salt and pepper. Heat the remaining 2 tablespoons olive oil in a medium-size nonstick skillet over medium heat. Add the salmon and cook, undisturbed, until browned on one side and just opaque in the center, about 5 minutes.
5. Place the lettuce leaves in the base of your serving bowl. Top with the farro, black beans and salmon. Garnish with the avocado, scallions and sliced chile; drizzle with the dressing.

Nutritional Value: 233 calories | 26g protein. | 15g fat | 30g carbohydrate | Fiber: 27g

HARISSA CHICKPEA STEW WITH EGGPLANT AND MILLET

PREP TIME: 10 MINS   **COOK TIME:** 45 MINS   **SERVINGS:** 2

The delightful fusion of smoky harissa, hearty chickpeas, and nutrient-rich ingredients not only tantalizes your taste buds but also keeps you satisfied and energized. It's a perfect choice for those seeking a high-fiber, plant-based delight.

INGREDIENTS

- 1 cup millet
- Kosher salt
- 2 tablespoons ghee (or another neutral high-heat oil), divided
- 1 large Japanese eggplant
- Freshly ground black pepper
- 1 onion, diced
- 3 garlic cloves, minced
- One 14-ounce can puréed tomatoes
- One 14-ounce can chickpeas, drained
- 2 tablespoons harissa paste
- 1 bunch cilantro, for garnish

DIRECTIONS

1. Fill a medium saucepan with 2 cups water and add the millet and a pinch of salt. Bring to a boil, cover, reduce to a simmer and cook for 25 minutes. Once the millet is done cooking, remove the lid, fluff with a fork and allow to cool.
2. Meanwhile, heat 1 tablespoon of ghee or oil in a deep skillet over medium heat. Add the eggplant, season with salt and pepper, and cook until tender and golden brown, adding more ghee as necessary to prevent the eggplant from sticking to the skillet, about 10 minutes. Transfer the eggplant to a bowl and set it aside.
3. Add the remaining 1 tablespoon of ghee or oil to the same skillet, add the onion and cook until soft and golden brown, 8 to 10 minutes.
4. Add the garlic and cook for 2 more minutes. Season with salt and pepper, and then add the tomatoes, chickpeas and harissa.
5. Return the eggplant to the skillet and reduce the heat to low; allow to simmer for 10 to 15 minutes.
6. Divide the millet between two bowls and top with the stew. Garnish with a few leaves of cilantro and serve warm.

Nutritional Value: 354 calories | 27g protein. | 20g fat | 44g carbohydrate | Fiber: 35g

LEMON-TAHINI SALAD WITH LENTILS, BEETS AND CARROTS

PREP TIME: 20 MINS   **COOK TIME:** 40 MINS   **SERVINGS:** 2

Elevate your daily fiber intake with our refreshing Lemon-Tahini Salad. Packed with nutrient-rich lentils, earthy beets, and vibrant carrots, this salad is not only a feast for your taste buds but also a fiber powerhouse. The zesty lemon-tahini dressing complements the natural flavors of these wholesome ingredients, making it a perfect choice for a satisfying and healthy meal.

INGREDIENTS

- 3 small beets, scrubbed
- ¾ cup small green lentils
- Kosher salt
- 3 tablespoons tahini
- 2 tablespoons fresh lemon juice
- 1 teaspoon honey
- Freshly ground pepper
- 1 small onion, finely chopped
- 2 lightly packed cups baby kale
- 1 romaine heart, chopped
- 1½ cups diced carrots

DIRECTIONS

1. Fill a deep skillet with ½ inch water and bring to a simmer over medium heat. Add the beets, cover, and cook until tender, about 20 minutes. Drain and run the beets under cold water to cool. Rub off the skins and then dice.
2. Meanwhile, in a small saucepan, combine the lentils and enough water to cover by 2 inches; bring to a boil over high heat.
3. Cover partially, reduce the heat to medium and simmer until the lentils are tender, 20 to 25 minutes. Season with salt and let stand 5 minutes, then drain off any excess water.
4. In a large bowl, whisk together the tahini, lemon juice, honey and 2 tablespoons water; season with salt and pepper. Add the onion and let stand 5 minutes.
5. Add the kale, romaine heart, carrots, beets and lentils; toss to combine and then season with salt and pepper.

Nutritional Value: 340 calories | 27g protein. | 12g fat | 34g carbohydrate | Fiber: 26g

CHICKEN AVOCADO BLACK BEAN SALAD

PREP TIME: 10 MINS   **COOK TIME:** 20 MINS   **SERVINGS:** 4

A Mexican-inspired salad with tender chicken, black beans, creamy avocado, juicy tomatoes, cilantro, lime juice and more! EASY, ready in 20 minutes, high-fiber, and packed with fiesta flavours galore!

INGREDIENTS

- 3 tablespoons olive oil
- 1 to 1.25 pounds boneless skinless chicken breast, diced into bite-sized pieces
- 1 tablespoon cumin
- 1 tablespoon chili powder, or to taste
- 3 to 4 cloves garlic, finely minced or pressed
- one 15-ounce can black beans, drained and rinsed (I use no-salt added)
- salt and freshly ground black pepper, to taste
- 2 cups cherry or grape tomatoes, halved
- 2 green onions, sliced into thin rounds
- 1 or 2 medium ripe Hass avocados, diced into medium chunks
- 1/3 cup fresh cilantro, or to taste
- 2 to 4 tablespoons freshly squeezed lime juice
- 2 tablespoons apple cider vinegar
- 1 to 3 teaspoons agave or honey, optional and to taste
- pinch cayenne pepper, optional and to taste

Nutritional Value: 351 calories | 26g protein. | 15g fat | 40g carbohydrate | Fiber: 25g

DIRECTIONS

1. To a large skillet, add the olive oil, chicken, evenly sprinkle with cumin and chili powder, and cook over medium-high heat until done, about 5 minutes.
2. Stir and flip intermittently to ensure even cooking. Add the garlic, stir to combine, and cook for about 1 minute, or until fragrant.
3. Add the black beans, stir to combine, evenly season everything with salt and pepper, and cook for about 1 minute, or until beans are lightly warmed.
4. Transfer skillet contents to a large bowl, add the tomatoes, green onions, avocado, cilantro, lime juice, apple cider vinegar, and stir to combine.
5. Check for seasoning balance, and if desired, add the optional agave/honey, optional cayenne, additional salt or pepper (I needed to add another 1 teaspoon of each), etc.

QUINOA BOWL WITH AVOCADO SAUCE

PREP TIME: 20 MINS **COOK TIME:** 40 MINS **SERVINGS:** 24

Quinoa bowl with Roasted Veggies and Avocado Sauce is made with oven roasted beets, sweet potatoes, cauliflower, asparagus and pan toasted chickpeas, served over a fluffy bed of quinoa and drizzled with a creamy and flavorful avocado dressing. The ultimate feel good meal.

INGREDIENTS

- 1 cup quinoa
- 2 teaspoons extra virgin olive oil
- 2 cups vegetable broth
- 3 beets peeled and cut into 1 inch cubes
- 1 large or 2 small sweet potatoes peeled and cut into 2 inch cubes
- 1 head cauliflower cut into florets
- 1 pound asparagus thick ends cut off
- salt to taste
- few tablespoons extra virgin olive oil
- 1 and 1/2 cups chickpeas

For the dressing:
- 1/2 avocado
- 2 tablespoons lemon juice
- 2 tablespoon extra virgin olive oil
- 1-2 cloves garlic minced
- 1/4 cup coconut milk
- 1/4 cup water or more depending on desired consistency
- salt to taste

DIRECTIONS

1. Preheat oven to 425 degrees F. Heat pot over medium heat, add 2 teaspoon olive oil and quinoa.
2. Toast for a few minutes until quinoa starting to brown. Add vegetable broth, bring to a boil, reduce heat and simmer, covered 15-20 minutes until quinoa cooked through.
3. Separately toss each of the veggies with a drizzle of olive oil (just to coat them) and salt to taste.
4. Place in single layer on baking sheet and roast in preheated oven until cooked through. The beets and sweet potatoes with need 40-45 minutes, the asparagus will need 20 minutes and the cauliflower will need 25 mins.
5. Heat pan over medium heat and add 1 teaspoon olive oil. Add chickpeas and toast until browned.
6. In a blender combine the ingredients for the dressing and process until smooth

Nutritional Value: 354 calories | 21g protein. | 20g fat | 34g carbohydrate | Fiber: 25g

CAULIFLOWER CHICKEN NACHOS

PREP TIME: 20 MINS **COOK TIME:** 40 MINS **SERVINGS:** 4

Savor the mouthwatering goodness of Cauliflower Chicken Nachos, a tasty twist on a classic favorite. This recipe not only tantalizes your taste buds with savory chicken and cheese but also adds a fiber boost by using cauliflower as the base. It's a guilt-free, crunchy delight that packs both flavor and nutrition into every bite, making it a perfect snack or appetizer for any occasion.

INGREDIENTS

- 3 tablespoons grapeseed oil or avocado oil
- ¾ teaspoon chili powder
- ¾ teaspoon ground cumin
- ¾ teaspoon onion powder
- ¼ teaspoon salt, divided
- 8 cups large cauliflower florets, cut into 1/2-inch-thick slices
- 1 cup chopped tomato
- 1 avocado, diced
- ¼ cup chopped fresh cilantro
- 2 tablespoons pickled jalapeño peppers or fresh jalapeño pepper slices
- 2 tablespoons finely chopped red onion
- ¾ cup canned reduced-sodium refried black beans
- 2 cups shredded cooked chicken
- ¾ cup shredded Mexican cheese blend
- ¾ cup finely shredded cabbage

Nutritional Value: 344 calories | 25g protein. | 15g fat | 35g carbohydrate | Fiber: 25g

DIRECTIONS

1. Preheat oven to 400 degrees F. Coat a large rimmed baking sheet with cooking spray. Combine oil, chili powder, cumin, onion powder and 1/8 teaspoon salt in a large bowl.
2. Add cauliflower and gently toss to coat. Spread the cauliflower in a single layer on the prepared pan. Bake until tender and starting to brown, 15 to 20 minutes.
3. Meanwhile, combine tomato, avocado, cilantro, jalapeños, onion and the remaining 1/8 teaspoon salt in a small bowl. Top the cauliflower with beans, chicken and cheese.
4. Bake until the cheese is melted, about 5 minutes.
   Serve the "nachos" topped with the salsa and cabbage.

LEMON-ROASTED VEGETABLE HUMMUS BOWLS

PREP TIME: 15 MINS   **COOK TIME:** 30 MINS   **SERVINGS:** 4

This colorful and nutritious dish features a vibrant array of roasted vegetables paired with creamy hummus, all drizzled with a zesty lemon dressing. It's a delightful, fiber-packed meal that's as satisfying as it is healthy, making it an ideal choice for those seeking a flavorful and wholesome dining experience.

INGREDIENTS

- 1 ½ cups cauliflower florets
- 1 ½ cups broccoli florets
- 2 cloves garlic, thinly sliced
- 1 tablespoon extra-virgin olive oil
- 1 teaspoon dried oregano
- ¼ teaspoon salt
- ¾ cup diced red bell pepper (1-inch)
- ¾ cup diced zucchini (1-inch)
- 2 teaspoons lemon zest
- 2 cups cooked tricolor quinoa, cooled
- 1 cup hummus (see Tip)
- 4 lemon wedges
- 1 medium avocado

DIRECTIONS

1. Preheat oven to 425 degrees F. Combine cauliflower, broccoli and garlic on a rimmed baking sheet. Drizzle with oil and sprinkle with oregano and salt; stir to coat. Roast for 10 minutes.
2. Add bell pepper and zucchini to the vegetables in the pan; stir to combine. Roast until the vegetables are crisp-tender and lightly browned, 10 to 15 minutes more.
3. Sprinkle lemon zest over the vegetables; set aside to cool before assembling bowls.
4. Divide the roasted vegetables among 4 single-serving containers. Top each with 1/2 cup quinoa and 1/4 cup hummus and add a lemon wedge to each container.
5. Seal the containers and refrigerate for up to 4 days. To serve, squeeze the lemon wedge over the bowl and top with one-fourth avocado, diced.

Nutritional Value: 355 calories | 21g protein. | 15g fat | 34g carbohydrate | Fiber: 25g

BROCCOLI WITH BALSAMIC MUSHROOMS

PREP TIME: 15 MINS   **COOK TIME:** 25 MINS   **SERVINGS:** 4

Elevate your plate with the irresistible combination of tender broccoli and savory balsamic mushrooms. This high-fiber, low-calorie dish not only tantalizes your taste buds but also nourishes your body with essential nutrients. It's a quick, healthy side that complements any meal with its rich, earthy flavors and fiber-packed goodness.

INGREDIENTS

- 1 pound broccoli, cut into 1-inch florets, stems peeled if desired
- 3 tablespoons extra-virgin olive oil, divided
- 8 ounces shiitake mushrooms, stems removed, caps sliced 1/2 inch thick (4 cups)
- 4 ounces baby bella mushrooms, quartered (2 cups)
- ¼ teaspoon salt
- 2 large cloves garlic, minced
- 2 tablespoons balsamic vinegar
- 1 tablespoon reduced-sodium tamari
- 1 tablespoon butter
- ¼ teaspoon crushed red pepper

DIRECTIONS

1. Cook broccoli in a pot of boiling water until just tender, 3 to 4 minutes. Drain. Heat 2 tablespoons oil in a large skillet over medium-high heat.
2. Add shiitakes and baby bellas, sprinkle with salt and cook, stirring often, until deeply brown in spots, 5 to 8 minutes.
3. Reduce heat to medium; add garlic and the remaining 1 tablespoon oil and cook, stirring, for 30 seconds. Add vinegar and tamari and cook for 30 seconds more.
4. Remove from heat; stir in butter, then add the broccoli and crushed red pepper and gently toss to combine.

Nutritional Value: 322 calories | 25g protein. | 15g fat | 35g carbohydrate | Fiber: 25g

ROASTED BUTTERNUT SQUASH SALAD WITH BURRATA

PREP TIME: 5 MINS   **COOK TIME:** 30 MINS   **SERVINGS:** 4

Elevate your salad game with this Roasted Butternut Squash Salad featuring creamy burrata cheese. Packed with high-fiber ingredients, the roasted butternut squash adds a delightful, nutty sweetness to this dish, making it a wholesome and satisfying choice for a wholesome meal.

INGREDIENTS

- 3 tablespoons extra-virgin olive oil, divided
- 1 teaspoon ground cumin
- 1 teaspoon paprika
- ½ teaspoon ground pepper, divided
- ¼ teaspoon salt, divided
- 4 cups cubed butternut squash
- 1 tablespoon minced shallot
- 1 tablespoon pomegranate molasses (see Tips)
- 1 tablespoon balsamic vinegar
- ½ teaspoon dried thyme
- 6 cups lightly packed baby arugula
- 1 burrata ball (3 3/4 ounces), sliced
- ¼ cup toasted chopped walnuts
- ¼ cup pomegranate seeds (see Tips) (Optional)

DIRECTIONS

1. Preheat oven to 400 degrees F. Combine 1 tablespoon oil, cumin, paprika, 1/4 teaspoon pepper and 1/8 teaspoon salt in a medium bowl.
2. Add squash; toss to coat. Spread on a large rimmed baking sheet and roast, stirring once, until tender, about 25 minutes.
3. Meanwhile, whisk shallot, molasses, vinegar, thyme and the remaining 2 tablespoons oil, 1/4 teaspoon pepper and 1/8 teaspoon salt in a small bowl.
4. When the squash has finished roasting, toss arugula with 2 tablespoons of the vinaigrette.
5. Transfer to a serving platter. Scatter the squash over the arugula and top with burrata slices.
6. Drizzle with the remaining 2 tablespoons dressing and sprinkle with walnuts and pomegranate seeds (if using).

Nutritional Value: 322 calories | 21g protein. | 10g fat | 35g carbohydrate | Fiber: 24g

KALE & SHAVED BRUSSELS SPROUTS SALAD WITH AVOCADO CAESAR DRESSING

PREP TIME: 20 MINS   **COOK TIME:** 40 MINS   **SERVINGS:** 4

Savor the crunch of fiber-rich kale and shaved Brussels sprouts in this refreshing salad, complemented by the creamy goodness of an Avocado Caesar Dressing. Packed with essential nutrients and dietary fiber, this vibrant dish not only tantalizes your taste buds but also contributes to your overall well-being. Enjoy a guilt-free, flavorful salad that's as nourishing as it is delicious.

INGREDIENTS

- 1 tablespoon unsalted butter
- ¼ cup whole-wheat panko breadcrumbs
- 1 small avocado (about 6 ounces), mashed
- 3 tablespoons fresh lemon juice
- 2 tablespoons grated Parmesan cheese
- 1 tablespoon white miso
- 2 cloves garlic, grated
- 1 teaspoon Dijon mustard
- 1 teaspoon ground pepper
- ¼ teaspoon salt
- ¼ cup extra-virgin olive oil
- 2 bunches lacinato kale (about 8 ounces each), stemmed and chopped
- 12 ounces fresh Brussels sprouts, trimmed and thinly sliced

DIRECTIONS

1. Melt butter in a medium nonstick skillet over medium heat. Cook, swirling the pan occasionally, until the butter turns golden brown and smells nutty, 2 to 3 minutes.
2. Stir in panko; cook, stirring constantly, until coated in butter and toasted, 1 to 2 minutes. Transfer to a paper-towel-lined bowl.
3. Process avocado, lemon juice, Parmesan, miso, garlic, mustard, pepper and salt in a mini food processor until combined, about 30 seconds.
4. Add oil; process until thickened and smooth, 30 seconds to 1 minute. Transfer to a large bowl.
5. Add kale to the bowl with the dressing. Using clean hands, massage the dressing into the kale to soften it, 1 to 2 minutes.
6. Add sliced Brussels sprouts and toss to combine. Top with the toasted breadcrumbs

Nutritional Value: 343 calories | 27g protein. | 15g fat | 35g carbohydrate | Fiber: 25g

FETA & OLIVE STUFFED EGGPLANT

PREP TIME: 20 MINS   **COOK TIME:** 35 MINS   **SERVINGS:** 4

Experience the delectable fusion of Mediterranean flavors and a generous dose of dietary fiber in this Feta & Olive Stuffed Eggplant. This dish not only tantalizes your taste buds but also provides the benefits of a fiber-rich, wholesome meal. The combination of creamy feta and briny olives nestled within tender eggplant creates a delightful, nutritious masterpiece that's as satisfying as it is healthy.

INGREDIENTS

- 2 large eggplants (about 1 pound each)
- 2 tablespoons extra-virgin olive oil, divided
- 1 medium red onion, finely chopped
- 1 tablespoon tomato paste
- ½ teaspoon ground cumin
- 2 cloves garlic, minced
- 1 cup canned no-salt-added diced tomatoes
- 1 medium red bell pepper
- ½ cup chopped fresh flat-leaf parsley
- ⅓ cup pitted Kalamata olives, quartered
- 1 tablespoon red-wine vinegar
- ¾ cup crumbled feta cheese
- Chopped fresh dill and oregano, for garnish

Nutritional Value: 351 calories | 24g protein. | 13g fat | 35g carbohydrate | Fiber: 25g

DIRECTIONS

1. Position rack in upper third of oven; preheat to 400 degrees F. Line a rimmed baking sheet with foil.
2. Cut each eggplant in half lengthwise. Using a spoon, scoop out flesh from the halves, leaving about 1/2-inch border on the sides and bottoms. Coarsely chop the flesh and set aside.
3. Drizzle the insides of the eggplant shells evenly with 1 tablespoon oil. Place the shells, cut-side up, on the prepared baking sheet and roast until tender, 20 to 25 minutes. Remove from oven and increase oven temperature to broil.
4. While the eggplant roasts, heat the remaining 1 tablespoon oil in a large skillet over medium-high heat. Add onion; cook, stirring often, until softened, 3 to 4 minutes.
5. Add tomato paste, cumin, and garlic; cook, stirring constantly, until fragrant, about 1 minute. Add tomatoes, bell pepper and the reserved chopped eggplant; cook, stirring occasionally, until the eggplant is tender, 8 to 10 minutes. Remove from heat; stir in parsley, olives and vinegar.
6. Divide the filling evenly among the eggplant shells; top each with 3 tablespoons feta. Broil until the cheese is melted and golden, 6 to 8 minutes. Sprinkle with fresh oregano and dill, if desired.

FRITTATA WITH ASPARAGUS, LEEK & RICOTTA

PREP TIME: 20 MINS   **COOK TIME:** 40 MINS   **SERVINGS:** 4

This Frittata with Asparagus, Leek & Ricotta not only tantalizes your taste buds but also provides a hearty dose of dietary fiber. With the fresh crunch of asparagus and the savory richness of leeks, all swirled in a creamy ricotta filling, this dish is a fiber-packed sensation that's as wholesome as it is delicious.

INGREDIENTS

- 8 large eggs
- ¼ cup crème fraîche
- ½ teaspoon salt
- ¼ teaspoon ground pepper
- 2 tablespoons extra-virgin olive oil
- 3 cups thinly sliced leeks (about 2 medium), rinsed well and patted dry
- 1 pound asparagus, trimmed and cut into 1-inch pieces
- ¼ cup part-skim ricotta
- 2 tablespoons pesto
- ¼ cup fresh basil

DIRECTIONS

1. Position rack in upper third of oven; preheat broiler. Whisk eggs, crème fraîche, salt and pepper in a medium bowl; set near the stove.
2. Heat oil in a large cast-iron skillet over medium-high heat. Add leeks and asparagus and cook, stirring frequently, until soft, 5 to 6 minutes.
3. Pour the egg mixture over the vegetables and cook, lifting the edges so uncooked egg can flow underneath, until nearly set, about 2 minutes.
4. Dollop ricotta and pesto on top and place the pan under the broiler until the eggs are slightly browned, 1 1/2 to 2 minutes.
5. Let stand for 3 minutes. Run a spatula around the edge of the frittata, then underneath, until you can slide or lift it out onto a cutting board or serving plate. Top with basil.

Nutritional Value: 344 calories | 25g protein. | 15g fat | 35g carbohydrate | Fiber: 25g

CHEESY MARINARA BEANS

PREP TIME: 20 MINS   **COOK TIME:** 40 MINS   **SERVINGS:** 3

This quick and comforting recipe combines the hearty satisfaction of beans with the irresistible allure of marinara sauce and a cheesy topping. It's a perfect way to add extra fiber to your diet while enjoying a flavorful and cheesy delight. Ideal for a satisfying, protein-rich meal that the whole family will love.

INGREDIENTS

- 2 tablespoons extra-virgin olive oil
- 1 medium onion, chopped
- 2 cloves garlic, minced
- ⅓ cup tomato paste
- ¼ cup dry white wine
- 1 28-ounce can no-salt-added whole peeled tomatoes, preferably San Marzano
- 3 cups cooked corona beans or two 15-ounce cans no-salt-added cannellini beans, rinsed
- 2 tablespoons chopped fresh basil, plus more for garnish
- 2 tablespoons chopped fresh oregano, plus more for garnish
- 2 tablespoons chopped fresh parsley, plus more for garnish
- 1 large egg, lightly beaten
- ⅔ cup whole-milk ricotta cheese
- ½ cup grated Parmesan cheese, divided
- 1 cup shredded fontina cheese

Nutritional Value: 344 calories | 25g protein. | 12g fat | 30g carbohydrate | Fiber: 25g

DIRECTIONS

1. Heat oil in a large broiler-safe skillet over medium-high heat. Add onion and cook, stirring occasionally, until softened, about 5 minutes.
2. Add garlic and cook, stirring, until fragrant, about 1 minute. Add tomato paste and cook, stirring, until it starts to darken, about 2 minutes. Add wine and cook, scraping up any browned bits, until thickened, about 1 minute.
3. Add tomatoes and their juice, crushing the tomatoes with your hand as you add them. Stir in beans, basil, oregano and parsley. Bring to a simmer. Reduce heat to maintain a simmer and cook, stirring occasionally, until thickened, 18 to 20 minutes.
4. Meanwhile, place rack in upper third of oven; preheat broiler to high. Combine egg, ricotta and 1/4 cup Parmesan in a small bowl.
5. Gently stir the ricotta mixture into the bean mixture. Sprinkle fontina and the remaining 1/4 cup Parmesan on top.
6. Broil until the cheese is melted, 2 to 3 minutes. Garnish with more herbs, if desired.

BROCCOLI & QUINOA CASSEROLE

PREP TIME: 20 MINS **COOK TIME:** 60 MINS **SERVINGS:** 4

Savor the wholesome goodness of our Broccoli & Quinoa Casserole, a delectable dish that's not only rich in flavor but also packed with dietary fiber. This casserole offers the perfect combination of nutty quinoa, tender broccoli, and a creamy cheese sauce.

INGREDIENTS

- 2 cups water
- 1 cup quinoa
- 1 tablespoon extra-virgin olive oil
- ½ teaspoon salt, divided
- 4 cups small broccoli florets and chopped stems
- 1 (15.5 ounce) can no-salt-added cannellini beans, rinsed
- 1 cup whole milk
- 1 cup whole-milk plain strained yogurt, such as Greek or skyr
- 2 tablespoons chopped fresh thyme, plus more for garnish
- 3 cloves garlic, finely chopped
- ¾ teaspoon ground pepper
- ½ teaspoon onion powder
- 2 cups shredded fontina cheese, divided

DIRECTIONS

1. Position oven rack 5 inches from broiler; preheat to 350°F. Lightly coat a 13-by-9-inch broiler-safe baking dish with cooking spray.
2. Combine water, quinoa, oil and 1/4 teaspoon salt in a large saucepan; bring to a boil over medium-high heat. Reduce heat to medium-low; cover and cook, undisturbed, for 10 minutes.
3. Add broccoli to the mixture (do not stir); cover and continue cooking until all the water is absorbed, about 5 minutes. Remove from heat; let stand, covered, for 5 minutes.
4. Transfer the quinoa mixture to a large bowl. Add beans, milk, yogurt, thyme, garlic, pepper, onion powder, 1 1/2 cups cheese and the remaining 1/4 teaspoon salt.
5. Gently stir until evenly combined. Spoon the mixture into the prepared baking dish. Sprinkle with the remaining 1/2 cup cheese.
6. Bake until heated through and the cheese is melted, about 15 minutes. Set oven to broil (without removing the dish). Broil until lightly browned, about 3 minutes.
7. Remove from oven; let cool for 5 minutes. Garnish with additional thyme, if desired.

Nutritional Value: 353 calories | 25g protein. | 15g fat | 35g carbohydrate | Fiber: 24g

PILED-HIGH VEGETABLE PITAS

PREP TIME: 10 MINS   **COOK TIME:** 20 MINS   **SERVINGS:** 4

Elevate your mealtime with Piled-High Vegetable Pitas, a wholesome and fiber-packed delight. These pita pockets are generously filled with a colorful array of fresh veggies, creating a crunchy and satisfying experience. With every bite, you'll savor the delicious taste and the nourishing goodness of high-fiber ingredients.

INGREDIENTS

- 1 tablespoon olive oil
- 1 cup canned no-salt-added chickpeas (garbanzo beans), rinsed and patted dry
- ½ teaspoon paprika
- ¼ teaspoon garlic powder
- ¼ teaspoon ground cumin
- ⅛ teaspoon ground pepper
- 2 cups Roasted Butternut Squash & Root Vegetables (see Associated Recipes)
- 1 1/3 cups Lemon-Roasted Mixed Vegetables (see Associated Recipes)
- 1 cup fresh baby spinach
- ½ cup cherry tomatoes, halved
- ¼ cup crumbled reduced-fat feta cheese (1 oz.)
- 2 (6 to 7 inch) whole-wheat pita bread rounds, halved horizontally and lightly toasted (see Tip)
- ½ cup hummus
- Lemon wedges

Nutritional Value: 343 calories | 25g protein. | 15g fat | 44g carbohydrate | Fiber: 24g

DIRECTIONS

1. Heat oil in a 10-inch skillet over medium heat. Add chickpeas; sprinkle with paprika, garlic powder, cumin, and pepper.
2. Cook, stirring frequently, until the chickpeas are lightly browned, 6 to 8 minutes. Transfer the chickpeas to a medium bowl.
3. Add Roasted Butternut Squash & Root Vegetables, Lemon-Roasted Mixed Vegetables, spinach, tomatoes, and feta; toss gently to combine. Serve with pita, hummus, and lemon wedges.

SUMMER VEGETABLE GNOCCHI SALAD

PREP TIME: 20 MINS　　**COOK TIME:** 40 MINS　　**SERVINGS:** 4

This Summer Vegetable Gnocchi Salad is not only a delicious and refreshing dish for hot days but also a fantastic source of dietary fiber. Packed with colorful, seasonal vegetables and soft potato gnocchi, it's a quick, fiber-rich, and flavorful option for a light and satisfying meal.

INGREDIENTS

- 1 (16 ounce) package whole-wheat gnocchi
- 1 small eggplant, sliced lengthwise into 1/2-inch planks
- 1 medium zucchini, sliced lengthwise into 1/2-inch planks
- 1 medium yellow squash, sliced lengthwise into 1/2-inch planks
- 1 ear corn, husked
- ½ medium red onion, cut into 1/2-inch-thick rings
- 4 tablespoons extra-virgin olive oil, divided
- 2 tablespoons balsamic vinegar
- 2 tablespoons chopped fresh basil
- 2 cloves garlic, grated
- ½ teaspoon ground pepper
- ¼ teaspoon salt
- ½ cup crumbled feta cheese

DIRECTIONS

1. Preheat grill to medium-high. Boil gnocchi according to package directions. Drain. Meanwhile, brush eggplant, zucchini, squash, corn and onion with 2 tablespoons oil.
2. Grill the vegetables, turning occasionally, until charred and tender, 6 to 10 minutes total. Transfer to a cutting board. Remove the corn kernels from the cob and cut the other vegetables into bite-size pieces.
3. Whisk the remaining 2 tablespoons oil, vinegar, basil, garlic, pepper and salt in a large bowl.
4. Add the gnocchi and the vegetables and toss to coat. Serve sprinkled with feta.

Nutritional Value: 344 calories | 25g protein. | 19g fat | 35g carbohydrate | Fiber: 25g

EGGPLANT CURRY

PREP TIME: 20 MINS　　**COOK TIME:** 25 MINS　　**SERVINGS:** 4

Savor the exquisite flavors of Eggplant Curry, a delectable dish that not only delights your taste buds but also offers a generous dose of dietary fiber. This savory and aromatic curry combines the tender goodness of eggplants with a medley of spices, providing a satisfying meal that's as wholesome as it is delicious.

INGREDIENTS

- 2 large eggplants (about 1 pound each), cut into 1-inch cubes (8 cups)
- ¼ teaspoon ground pepper
- 3 tablespoons olive oil, divided
- 1 ½ teaspoons kosher salt, divided
- 2 cups chopped white onion
- 1 tablespoon red curry paste
- 3 medium cloves garlic, grated
- 1 (1/2 inch) piece fresh ginger, peeled and grated
- 3 medium plum tomatoes, diced (about 2 cups)
- 1 (15 ounce) can no-salt-added chickpeas, rinsed
- 1 (15 ounce) can light coconut milk, well shaken
- 4 cups cooked brown rice
- Fresh cilantro and lime wedges for serving

Nutritional Value: 314 calories | 26g protein. | 15g fat | 30g carbohydrate | Fiber: 25g

DIRECTIONS

1. Preheat oven to 450 degrees F. Line a large rimmed baking sheet with foil. Toss eggplant, pepper, 2 tablespoons oil and 1/4 teaspoon salt on the prepared baking sheet.
2. Roast until the eggplant is tender, about 20 minutes. Meanwhile, heat the remaining 1 tablespoon oil in a skillet over medium-high heat. Add onion; cook, stirring often, until just softened, about 3 minutes.
3. Stir in curry paste, garlic and ginger; cook, stirring often, until fragrant, about 30 seconds. Stir in tomatoes, chickpeas, coconut milk and the remaining 1 1/4 teaspoons salt.
4. Bring to a boil over medium-high heat; reduce heat to medium-low and simmer until the sauce has reduced and thickened slightly, about 15 minutes.
5. Stir the roasted eggplant into the curry mixture. Serve over cooked rice with cilantro and lime wedges.

GRILLED CAULIFLOWER STEAKS WITH ALMOND PESTO & BUTTER BEANS

PREP TIME: 20 MINS   **COOK TIME:** 30 MINS   **SERVINGS:** 4

Elevate your meal with Grilled Cauliflower Steaks with Almond Pesto & Butter Beans - a delectable dish that not only tantalizes your taste buds but also provides a healthy dose of fiber. This savory and satisfying recipe features hearty cauliflower steaks, a flavorful almond pesto, and creamy butter beans, all grilled to perfection.

INGREDIENTS

- ½ cup almonds
- 5 tablespoons chopped flat-leaf parsley, divided, plus more for garnish
- ¼ cup packed fresh basil, plus more for garnish
- 2 tablespoons chopped fresh chives, plus more for garnish
- Zest & juice of 1 lemon
- 5 tablespoons extra-virgin olive oil, divided
- 1 teaspoon salt, divided
- 2 large heads cauliflower
- 2 teaspoons smoked paprika
- 1 teaspoon garlic powder
- 2 medium shallots, minced
- 1 clove garlic, minced
- 2 (15 ounce) cans no-salt-added butter beans, rinsed
- ½ cup water
- ¼ teaspoon ground pepper
- 2 teaspoons sherry vinegar

Nutritional Value: 342 calories | 25g protein. | 15g fat | 35g carbohydrate | Fiber: 25g

DIRECTIONS

1. Preheat grill to medium. Pulse almonds, 4 tablespoons parsley, basil, chives, lemon zest and juice, 2 tablespoons oil and 1/4 teaspoon salt in a food processor until chopped.
2. Place cauliflower heads on a cutting board, stem-side down. Using a large chef's knife, cut two 1/2-inch-thick slices from the center of each head to make 4 "steaks."
3. (Reserve the remaining cauliflower for another use.) Brush the steaks with 2 tablespoons oil. Combine paprika, garlic powder and 1/2 teaspoon salt in a small bowl. Sprinkle the mixture on both sides of the steaks.
4. Grill the steaks, turning once, until tender and nicely charred, 12 to 14 minutes total.
5. Meanwhile, heat the remaining 1 tablespoon oil in a medium saucepan over medium heat. Add shallots and garlic and cook until the shallots start to soften, about 1 minute. Add beans, water, pepper and the remaining 1/4 teaspoon salt.
6. Cook, stirring occasionally, until hot, about 5 minutes. Remove from heat and stir in vinegar and the remaining 1 tablespoon parsley.
7. Serve the cauliflower steaks over the beans, topped with the pesto and more herbs, if desired.

BLACK BEAN BULGUR SALAD

PREP TIME: 20 MINS   **COOK TIME:** 30 MINS   **SERVINGS:** 4

A refreshing and healthy salad packed with protein and fiber from black beans and bulgur wheat. It's a great vegetarian lunch option that's also customizable with various vegetables and dressings

INGREDIENTS

- 1 cup bulgur
- 2 cups vegetable broth
- 1/4 cup orange juice
- 1/4 cup lime juice
- 1 jalapeno pepper, seeded and minced
- 2 tablespoons olive oil
- 1/4 teaspoon ground cumin
- 1 cup shredded carrots
- 3 tablespoons minced fresh cilantro
- 1 can (15 ounces) black beans, rinsed and drained
- 1 cup frozen corn, thawed
- 3/4 cup shredded Monterey Jack cheese
- Sliced jalapeno pepper, optional

DIRECTIONS

1. Place bulgur and broth in a small saucepan; bring to a boil. Reduce heat; simmer, covered, until tender, 12-15 minutes.
2. Transfer to a large bowl; cool slightly. For dressing, whisk together citrus juices, minced jalapeno, oil and cumin. Add 1/3 cup dressing to bulgur; stir in carrots and cilantro.
3. To serve, divide bulgur mixture among 4 bowls. Top with beans, corn, cheese and, if desired, sliced jalapeno. Drizzle with remaining dressing.

Nutritional Value: 350 calories | 25g protein. | 15g fat | 30g carbohydrate | Fiber: 24g

CRAB LOUIE SALAD

PREP TIME: 20 MINS   **COOK TIME:** 40 MINS   **SERVINGS:** 4

Savor the sumptuousness of a Crab Louie Salad, a classic dish brimming with flavors and textures. Beyond its delightful combination of crab, fresh veggies, and tangy dressing, this salad is also an excellent source of dietary fiber. This not only tantalizes your taste buds but also keeps you feeling full and satisfied. A perfect choice for a healthy and satisfying meal that's both delicious and nutritious.

INGREDIENTS

Dressing
- ½ cup ketchup
- ½ cup mayonnaise
- ¼ cup minced yellow onion
- 1 clove garlic, minced
- 1 tablespoon dill pickle relish
- 2 teaspoons dried dill
- 1 teaspoon prepared horseradish
- 1 teaspoon lemon juice

Salad
- 8 asparagus spears, trimmed
- 1 medium head green-leaf lettuce, torn
- 2 medium tomatoes, cut into wedges
- 2 hard-boiled eggs, quartered
- 2 stalks celery, sliced
- 1 ripe avocado, sliced
- ½ medium cucumber, sliced
- 2 scallions, sliced
- ½ cup sliced canned pitted black olives, rinsed
- ¼ cup sliced red onion
- 6 ounces cooked crabmeat
- Lemon wedges for serving

Nutritional Value: 322 calories | 25g protein. | 15g fat | 35g carbohydrate | Fiber: 25g

DIRECTIONS

1. To prepare dressing: Whisk ketchup, mayonnaise, yellow onion, garlic, relish, dill, horseradish and lemon juice in a medium bowl.
2. To prepare salad: Bring 1 inch of water to a boil in a large pot fitted with a steamer basket. Place a bowl of ice water near the stove. Add asparagus to the pot, cover and steam until tender-crisp, 3 to 5 minutes. Transfer to the ice bath. Drain and pat dry.
3. Place lettuce on a serving platter. Arrange the asparagus, tomatoes, eggs, celery, avocado, cucumber, scallions, olives and red onion on top.
4. Top with crabmeat and dollop with half the dressing (reserve the remaining dressing for another use). Serve with lemon wedges, if desired.

SUCCOTASH SALAD WITH GRILLED SIRLOIN

PREP TIME: 15 MINS **COOK TIME:** 40 MINS **SERVINGS:** 4

Elevate your taste buds and boost your fiber intake with this Succotash Salad featuring succulent grilled sirloin. This refreshing salad combines the wholesome goodness of lima beans, corn, and other vibrant veggies, providing a satisfying dose of dietary fiber while delivering the savory delight of perfectly grilled sirloin.

INGREDIENTS

- 2 cups green beans, trimmed and cut into 1-inch pieces
- 2 ears corn, shucked
- ½ cup whole-milk plain Greek yogurt
- 3 tablespoons fresh lime juice
- 2 tablespoons minced red onion
- 2 tablespoons olive oil, divided
- 2 teaspoons honey
- 1 ½ teaspoons minced garlic
- 1 ¼ teaspoons ground pepper, divided
- 1 teaspoon salt, divided
- 1 tablespoon chili powder
- 1 tablespoon ground cumin
- 2 teaspoons garlic powder
- 1 pound sweet potatoes (2 medium), peeled and cut into 1/4-inch planks
- 1 pound top sirloin steak, trimmed
- 1 cup halved cherry tomatoes
- 1 cup frozen lima beans, thawed
- ¼ cup chopped fresh basil
- ¼ cup chopped fresh cilantro
- 1 jalapeño pepper, seeded and minced

Nutritional Value: 333 calories | 25g protein. | 15g fat | 35g carbohydrate | Fiber: 25g

DIRECTIONS

1. Bring 3/4 cup water to a boil in a large skillet over medium-high heat. Add green beans; cover, reduce heat to medium-low and steam for 5 minutes. Drain and transfer to a large bowl.
2. Fill the now-empty skillet with 2 inches of water and bring to a boil. Add corn to the boiling water; cover, turn off heat, and steam for 8 minutes. Drain the corn and transfer to a cutting board; let cool. Cut the kernels from the cobs and transfer to the bowl with the green beans.
3. Meanwhile, whisk yogurt, lime juice, onion, 1 Tbsp. oil, honey, garlic, and 1/4 tsp. each pepper and salt in a small bowl.
4. Combine chili powder, cumin, garlic powder, and the remaining 1 tsp. ground pepper and 3/4 tsp. salt in a small bowl.
5. Preheat grill to medium-high (see Tip). Clean the grill grate with a long-handled wire brush.
6. Brush both sides of sweet potatoes with the remaining 1 Tbsp. oil, then season with half of the spice mixture. Rub the remaining spice mixture all over steak. Grill the sweet potatoes until fork-tender, 3 to 5 minutes per side. Grill the steak to the desired degree of doneness (135 degrees F for medium-rare), 3 to 5 minutes per side.
7. Transfer the sweet potatoes to a clean cutting board and let cool. Transfer the steak to a clean cutting board and let rest for 5 minutes.
8. When cool enough to handle, cut the sweet potatoes into 1-inch pieces. Cut the steak into 1/2-inch-thick slices.
9. Add the sweet potatoes to the bowl with the green beans and corn. Stir in tomatoes, lima beans, basil, cilantro, and jalapeño; toss with 1/2 cup of the yogurt dressing.
10. Divide the salad among 4 plates. Divide the steak among the plates and drizzle with the remaining 1/4 cup yogurt dressing.

WHITE BEAN & VEGGIE SALAD

PREP TIME: 10 MINS   **COOK TIME:** 20 MINS   **SERVINGS:** 1

Elevate your nutrition with this White Bean & Veggie Salad – a vibrant and fiber-packed dish that's as wholesome as it is delicious. Loaded with colorful vegetables and hearty white beans, this salad is a refreshing way to boost your daily fiber intake while savoring a burst of natural flavors.

INGREDIENTS

- 2 cups mixed salad greens
- ¾ cup veggies of your choice, such as chopped cucumbers and cherry tomatoes
- ⅓ cup canned white beans, rinsed and drained
- ½ avocado, diced
- 1 tablespoon red-wine vinegar
- 2 teaspoons extra-virgin olive oil
- ¼ teaspoon kosher salt
- Freshly ground pepper to taste

DIRECTIONS

1. Combine greens, veggies, beans and avocado in a medium bowl.
2. Drizzle with vinegar and oil and season with salt and pepper. Toss to combine and transfer to a large plate.

Nutritional Value: 322 calories | 21g protein. | 25g fat | 30g carbohydrate | Fiber: 25g

EGG, SPINACH & CHEDDAR SANDWICH

PREP TIME: 10 MINS   **COOK TIME:** 20 MINS   **SERVINGS:** 1

Savor the wholesome goodness of the Egg, Spinach & Cheddar Sandwich, a fiber-rich delight that combines the protein-packed richness of eggs with the vibrant flavors of fresh spinach and melted cheddar. This delectable sandwich not only satiates your taste buds but also provides a healthy dose of fiber, making it a perfect choice for a nourishing and fulfilling breakfast or brunch option.

INGREDIENTS

- 2 teaspoons extra-virgin olive oil, divided
- 2 cups coarsely chopped baby spinach
- ½ teaspoon garlic powder
- ¼ teaspoon ground pepper, divided
- ⅛ teaspoon salt
- 1 large egg
- 1 whole-grain English muffin, toasted
- 2 tablespoons shredded extra-sharp Cheddar cheese

DIRECTIONS

1. Heat 1 teaspoon oil in a medium nonstick skillet over medium heat. Add spinach, garlic powder, 1/8 teaspoon pepper and salt; cook, stirring, until the spinach is wilted, 1 to 2 minutes. Transfer to a plate.
2. Add the remaining 1 teaspoon oil to the pan. Break egg into the pan; sprinkle with the remaining 1/8 teaspoon pepper.
3. Cook until set on the bottom, 1 to 2 minutes. Break the yolk, then flip the egg and cook, undisturbed, until set, about 1 minute more.
4. Place the spinach on an English muffin half. Sprinkle with cheese, then top with the fried egg and remaining muffin half.

Nutritional Value: 353 calories | 21g protein. | 20g fat | 30g carbohydrate | Fiber: 25g

BUTTERY SHRIMP WITH MARINATED WHITE BEANS

PREP TIME: 20 MINS **COOK TIME:** 40 MINS **SERVINGS:** 4

This dish is a delightful combination of textures and flavors. Plump, juicy shrimp are cooked in a buttery sauce that's bursting with garlic and lemon. The accompanying marinated white beans add a creamy contrast and a boost of protein. A sprinkle of fresh parsley brings a touch of brightness to the whole dish, making it both satisfying and impressive.

INGREDIENTS

- 2 large lemons
- 2 15-oz. cans cannellini beans, drained and rinsed
- 5 tablespoons olive oil, divided
- 1 ¼ teaspoons kosher salt, divided
- 4 large cloves garlic, finely chopped (about 2 Tbsp.)
- ¼ teaspoon crushed red pepper
- 3 tablespoons unsalted butter, divided
- ¼ cup dry white wine
- 1 pound peeled, deveined large shrimp
- ⅓ cup chopped fresh parsley leaves
- Toasted bread, for serving (optional)

DIRECTIONS

1. Remove lemon peel in wide strips with a vegetable peeler, avoiding white pith.
2. Finely chop strips to equal 1 tablespoon; transfer to a medium bowl. Squeeze lemons to equal 3½ tablespoons juice.
3. Add beans, 3 tablespoons oil, ¾ teaspoon salt, and 2 tablespoons lemon juice to chopped lemon peel in bowl.
4. Place garlic, crushed red pepper, 2 tablespoons butter, and remaining tablespoons oil in a large skillet. Cook over medium, stirring often, until garlic is lightly golden, about 4 minutes. Add wine and cook until reduced by half, about 1 minute.
5. Add shrimp and increase heat to medium-high. Cook until shrimp are just opaque, 3 to 4 minutes. Stir in parsley and remaining 1½ tablespoons lemon juice, ½ teaspoon salt, and 1 tablespoon butter. Serve over beans with bread, if using.

Nutritional Value: 310 calories | 29g protein. | 27g fat | 34g carbohydrate | Fiber: 25g

POT CHICKEN SAUSAGE AND BEANS

PREP TIME: 20 MINS **COOK TIME:** 40 MINS **SERVINGS:** 4

This one-pot dish combines flavorful chicken sausage, tender beans, and your favorite vegetables in a rich broth for a satisfying and easy meal.

INGREDIENTS

- ¼ cup olive oil, divided
- 1 12-oz. package andouille chicken sausage, pricked with a fork
- 1 cup panko
- 1 ¼ teaspoon kosher salt, divided
- 1 yellow onion, chopped
- 1 carrot, grated
- 4 cloves garlic, crushed
- 1 pound ground pork
- ½ teaspoon freshly ground black pepper
- 2 tablespoons tomato paste
- 1 14.5-oz. can crushed tomatoes
- 2 sprigs thyme, plus leaves for serving
- 2 15.5-oz. cans cannellini beans, drained and rinsed

DIRECTIONS

1. Heat 2 tablespoons oil in a large, heavy-bottomed pot or Dutch oven over medium.
2. Add sausage; cook, turning often, until browned on all sides, about 8 minutes. Transfer to a plate. Add panko and ¼ teaspoon salt to pot; cook, stirring constantly, until golden, about 2 minutes.
3. Transfer to a bowl. Wipe pot clean. Heat remaining 2 tablespoons oil over medium. Add onion, carrot, and garlic; cook, stirring often, until softened, about 5 minutes.
4. Increase heat to medium-high. Add ground pork, pepper, and remaining 1 teaspoon salt; cook, breaking up pork with a wooden spoon and stirring occasionally, until browned, 6 to 8 minutes.
5. Add tomato paste; cook until darkened and coating pork, about 2 minutes. Stir in 1¾ cups water, crushed tomatoes, and thyme, scraping up browned bits; bring to a boil.
6. Reduce heat to medium-low. Simmer, stirring often, until sauce thickens slightly, about 10 minutes. Meanwhile, diagonally slice sausage.
7. Add beans and sliced sausage to pot. Cook over medium, stirring occasionally, until warmed through, about 2 minutes.
8. Discard thyme sprigs. Sprinkle with panko and thyme leaves before serving.

Nutritional Value: 344 calories | 25g protein. | 15g fat | 35g carbohydrate | Fiber: 25g

CREAMY SWISS CHARD GRATIN WITH CRISPY GNOCCHI

PREP TIME: 10 MINS

COOK TIME: 50 MINS

SERVINGS: 4

Savor the delectable goodness of this Creamy Swiss Chard Gratin with Crispy Gnocchi, a dish that's not only a treat for your taste buds but also a fantastic source of dietary fiber. The creamy Swiss chard is perfectly complemented by the crispy, golden-brown gnocchi, creating a dish that's both comforting and nutritious.

INGREDIENTS

- 1.50 pounds Swiss chard (about 3 bunches)
- ¼ cup unsalted butter, divided
- ¼ cup extra-virgin olive oil, divided
- 2 (12-ounces) pkg. refrigerated potato gnocchi (such as Giovanni Rana Skillet Gnocchi), divided
- 1.50 teaspoon kosher salt, divided
- ¾ teaspoon black pepper, divided
- 1 large red onion (about 12 ounces), thinly sliced (about 2 1/2 cups)
- 3 cup all-purpose flour (about 1 1/2 ounces)
- 3 ¼ cups whole milk
- 2 ounces Gruyère cheese, shredded (about 1/2 cup)
- 2 ounces Parmigiano-Reggiano cheese, grated (about 1/2 cup)
- 1.50 tablespoons Dijon mustard
- 1 teaspoon grated garlic
- ¼ teaspoon cayenne pepper
- ¼ teaspoon ground nutmeg

Nutritional Value: 352 calories | 24g protein. | 15g fat | 35g carbohydrate | Fiber: 25g

DIRECTIONS

1. Preheat oven to 375°F with rack 10 inches from heat. Bring a large pot of salted water to a boil over high.
2. Remove stems from Swiss chard; trim and discard stem ends, and thinly slice remaining stems. Slice chard leaves into 1-inch-thick strips. Add leaves and stems to boiling water; cook, stirring often, until leaves are wilted and stems are crisp-tender, 1 to 2 minutes.
3. Drain well in a colander. Let cool 15 minutes. Gently squeeze over sink to remove any excess liquid. Set aside.
4. Wipe pot clean. Add 1 tablespoon butter and 1 tablespoon oil; cook over medium-high until butter melts. Add 1 package of gnocchi; cook, turning gnocchi occasionally, until golden brown and crisp, 5 to 7 minutes. Transfer to a baking sheet.
5. Repeat process with 1 tablespoon butter, 1 tablespoon oil, and remaining gnocchi. Season all gnocchi with 1/2 teaspoon salt and 1/4 teaspoon black pepper. Set aside.
6. Add remaining 2 tablespoons butter and remaining 2 tablespoons oil to pot; cook over medium until butter melts. Add onion; season with 1/4 teaspoon salt and 1/4 teaspoon black pepper. Cook, stirring occasionally, until onion is softened and translucent, about 8 minutes.
7. Sprinkle onion mixture with flour; cook over medium, stirring constantly, 2 minutes. Gradually whisk in milk until smooth. Bring just to a simmer over medium-high, whisking occasionally.
8. Reduce heat to low; gently simmer, whisking often, until mixture is thickened, about 5 minutes. Remove from heat. Stir in Gruyère, Parmigiano-Reggiano, mustard, garlic, cayenne, and nutmeg.
9. Fold in gnocchi and chard. Season with remaining 3/4 teaspoon salt and remaining 1/4 teaspoon black pepper. Spread mixture evenly into an 11- x 7-inch broiler-safe baking dish; place baking dish on a baking sheet lined with parchment paper to catch drips.
10. Bake in preheated oven until bubbling around edges, 20 to 25 minutes. Increase oven temperature to broil. (Do not remove baking dish from oven.) Broil until browned in spots, about 4 minutes. Remove from oven; let cool 5 minutes.

CHARRED CAULIFLOWER TACOS WITH ROMESCO SALSA

PREP TIME: 15 MINS   **COOK TIME:** 40 MINS   **SERVINGS:** 4

Elevate your taco night with these Charred Cauliflower Tacos topped with zesty Romesco Salsa. Not only are they a flavorful delight, but they're also a fantastic source of dietary fiber, thanks to the hearty cauliflower and nutrient-packed salsa.

INGREDIENTS

- Romesco Salsa
- 3 medium-size red bell peppers
- 1 (3 1/2-ounce) plum tomato
- ¾ cup toasted pecan halves
- ½ bunch fresh cilantro
- 3 large garlic cloves
- 3 tablespoons fresh lemon juice
- 2 tablespoons red wine vinegar
- 1 tablespoon smoked paprika
- ½ teaspoon cayenne pepper
- ½ cup extra-virgin olive oil
- 1 tablespoon kosher salt
- Tacos
- 1 medium head cauliflower, cut into 1 1/2-inch florets (about 6 cups)
- ¼ cup canola oil
- 12 (6-inch) blue corn tortillas, warmed
- 4 ounces queso fresco, crumbled (about 1 cup)
- 1 cup loosely packed fresh cilantro leaves
- 2 tablespoons toasted pine nuts
- 1 tablespoon cold-pressed extra-virgin olive oil
- Flaky sea salt (such as Maldon), for sprinkling
- 1 lime, cut into wedges

Nutritional Value: 314 calories | 21g protein. | 10g fat | 35g carbohydrate | Fiber: 24g

DIRECTIONS

1. Make the Romesco Salsa Preheat oven to broil with oven rack about 6 inches from heat. Place bell peppers and tomato on a large rimmed baking sheet. Broil, turning twice, until charred on all sides, 10 to 15 minutes.
2. Transfer charred peppers to a bowl, and cover with plastic wrap; let stand 30 minutes.
3. Remove skin from tomato; quarter tomato. Remove skin, seeds, and stem from bell peppers. Process bell peppers, tomato, pecans, cilantro, garlic, lemon juice, vinegar, smoked paprika, and cayenne in a blender until smooth, about 2 minutes.
4. With blender running on low speed, gradually add oil; process until smooth, about 30 seconds. Stir in salt.
Make the Tacos
5. Preheat oven to high broil with oven rack about 6 inches from heat. Toss together cauliflower florets and canola oil on a large rimmed baking sheet.
6. Broil, stirring twice, until cauliflower is browned, 10 to 15 minutes.
7. Top each tortilla with about 1/4 cup roasted cauliflower, 2 tablespoons romesco salsa, and 1 tablespoon queso fresco.
8. Garnish with cilantro and pine nuts, and finish with olive oil, a sprinkle of flaky sea salt, and a squeeze of lime juice.

FARRO SALAD WITH ROASTED ROOT VEGETABLES

PREP TIME: 20 MINS   **COOK TIME:** 40 MINS   **SERVINGS:** 4

Savor the hearty goodness of our Farro Salad with Roasted Root Vegetables, a fiber-packed dish that combines the wholesome nuttiness of farro with the earthy sweetness of roasted root vegetables. This vibrant and nutritious salad is a celebration of flavors and textures, making it an excellent choice for those looking to embrace a fiber-rich and satisfying meal.

INGREDIENTS

- 3 cups water
- 4 1/2 teaspoons kosher salt, divided, plus more to taste
- 1 1/2 cups uncooked pearled farro (about 9 1/4 ounces)
- 3 medium carrots, peeled and cut into 3/4-inch pieces (about 1 1/2 cups)
- 3 medium parsnips, peeled, cores removed and discarded, and cut into 3/4-inch pieces (about 1 1/2 cups)
- 1 small yellow onion, cut into 3/4-inch pieces (about 2 cups)
- 1 1/2 cups chopped peeled celery root (about 3/4-inch piece)
- 6 tablespoons extra-virgin olive oil, divided
- 1/4 cup chopped fresh flat-leaf parsley, plus parsley leaves, for garnish
- 3 tablespoons red wine vinegar, plus more to taste
- 1/2 teaspoon black pepper, plus more to taste

DIRECTIONS

1. Preheat oven to 450°F. Bring 3 cups water and 2 teaspoons salt to a boil in a large saucepan over medium-high. Stir in farro. Cover and reduce heat to low. Cook until farro is tender and water is mostly absorbed, 25 to 30 minutes.
2. Remove from heat, and let stand, covered, 10 minutes. While farro cooks, toss together carrots, parsnips, onion, celery root, 1/4 cup oil, and 2 teaspoons salt on a rimmed baking sheet; spread in an even layer. Roast in preheated oven until vegetables are tender and lightly browned, 25 to 30 minutes.
3. Drain any excess water from farro. Stir together farro, chopped parsley, vinegar, pepper, roasted vegetables and any residual oil from roasting pan, and remaining 1/2 teaspoon salt in a large bowl.
4. Let stand at room temperature at least 15 minutes or up to 3 hours, or cover and refrigerate up to 3 days. If chilled, let stand at room temperature 30 minutes before serving.
5. Just before serving, stir in remaining 2 tablespoons oil. Season to taste with salt, pepper, and vinegar. Garnish with parsley leaves.

Nutritional Value: 333 calories | 25g protein. | 10g fat | 35g carbohydrate | Fiber: 25g

EGGPLANT AND LENTIL STEW WITH POMEGRANATE MOLASSES

PREP TIME: 20 MINS   **COOK TIME:** 40 MINS   **SERVINGS:** 4

This hearty stew is not only a feast for your taste buds but also a fantastic source of dietary fiber, thanks to the lentils and eggplant. The drizzle of pomegranate molasses adds a delightful twist to this wholesome and satisfying dish, making it a must-try for those seeking a nutritious, plant-based meal with a touch of Middle Eastern flair.

INGREDIENTS

- One 1 1/2-pound long, narrow eggplant
- Salt
- 1/2 cup lentils
- Water
- 2/3 cup extra-virgin olive oil
- 1 medium onion, finely chopped
- 4 medium garlic cloves, minced
- 2 medium tomatoes, chopped
- 2 long green chiles, such as Anaheims—stemmed, seeded and coarsely chopped
- 2 tablespoons chopped mint leaves
- 1 tablespoon tomato paste
- 1/4 teaspoon crushed red pepper
- 1/4 cup pomegranate molasses

DIRECTIONS

1. Partially peel the eggplant so it has lengthwise stripes, then cut it lengthwise into 4 slices.
2. Score each slice on 1 side in a crosshatch pattern. Cut each slice crosswise into 3 pieces and set on a rimmed baking sheet. Sprinkle with salt. Let stand for 1 hour.
3. Meanwhile, in a small saucepan, cover the lentils with 2 inches of water and bring to a boil. Reduce the heat to moderate and simmer until tender, about 15 minutes. Drain the lentils.
4. Coat a small enameled cast-iron casserole with 1 tablespoon of the olive oil. In a bowl, toss the onion with the garlic, tomatoes, green chiles, mint, tomato paste, crushed red pepper and 2 teaspoons of salt.
5. Rinse the eggplant and pat dry. Spread 1/2 cup of the vegetable mixture in the casserole and top with half of the eggplant. Cover with half of the lentils and half of the remaining vegetable mixture. Top with the remaining eggplant, lentils and vegetables.
6. Pour the remaining olive oil around the side and over the vegetables, then drizzle with the pomegranate molasses.
7. Bring the stew to a boil. Cover and cook over low heat until the eggplant is very tender, about 1 1/2 hours. Serve hot, warm or at room temperature.

Nutritional Value: 344 calories | 25g protein. | 15g fat | 30g carbohydrate | Fiber: 24g

TAGLIATELLE WITH TOMATOES AND GREENS

PREP TIME: 15 MINS   **COOK TIME:** 35 MINS   **SERVINGS:** 4

This Tagliatelle with Tomatoes and Greens recipe is a delightful way to enjoy a fiber-packed, Italian-inspired dish. The tender tagliatelle pasta perfectly complements the vibrant mix of tomatoes and greens, making it a quick and healthy option for any meal. It's a flavorful, fiber-rich delight that you'll want to savor again and again.

INGREDIENTS

- 1 tablespoon (15 mL) extra-virgin olive oil
- 1 medium shallot, chopped
- 1½ cups (375 mL) chopped carrots
- 3 garlic cloves, minced
- 1 teaspoon (5 mL) dried oregano
- ¼ teaspoon (1 mL) red pepper flakes
- ¼ cup (60 mL) dry white wine
- 1 tablespoon (15 mL) balsamic vinegar
- 1 can (14.5 ounces/411 g) diced tomatoes
- 4 ounces (125 g) tagliatelle pasta
- 2 cups (500 mL) chopped kale leaves
- ½ cup (125 mL) cooked cannellini beans
- ¼ cup (60 mL) pine nuts
- 2 teaspoons (10 mL) capers
- Chopped chives or other herbs (basil, parsley, etc.)
- Sea salt and freshly ground black pepper
- Grated Parmesan cheese (optional)

DIRECTIONS

1. In a large pot, heat the olive oil over medium heat. Add the shallot and a pinch of salt and pepper and cook until soft, about 2 minutes. Add the carrots, garlic, oregano, red pepper flakes, and another few pinches of salt.
2. Let cook, stirring occasionally, until the vegetables are lightly browned, about 5 minutes.
3. Add the white wine. Stir and let the wine cook off until it's nearly evaporated, about 30 seconds. Add the balsamic vinegar and tomatoes. Cover and reduce the heat to a simmer. Cook until the carrots are tender, about 15 minutes.
4. Meanwhile, bring a medium pot of salted water to a boil. Prepare the pasta according to the instructions on the package, cooking until al dente. Drain the pasta.
5. Stir the chopped kale into the sauce and let it wilt down, about 1 minute. Add the pasta, cannellini beans, pine nuts, capers, and chives or herbs and toss gently to combine.
6. Season to taste with salt and pepper and serve with freshly grated Parmesan cheese, if desired.

Nutritional Value: 343 calories | 25g protein. | 15g fat | 30g carbohydrate | Fiber: 25g

REFRIED BEAN TOSTADAS

PREP TIME: 15 MINS   **COOK TIME:** 30 MINS   **SERVINGS:** 4

Savor the crunch and deliciousness of Refried Bean Tostadas, a dish that not only tantalizes your taste buds but also packs a fiber punch. These tostadas are a perfect combination of crispy tortillas topped with hearty, fiber-rich refried beans, and a medley of fresh, vibrant toppings. Get ready for a quick and wholesome meal that's as nutritious as it is flavorful.

INGREDIENTS

- 6 flour tortillas (8 inches)
- 1/2 pound sliced fresh mushrooms
- 1 cup diced zucchini
- 2 tablespoons canola oil
- 1 jar (16 ounces) chunky salsa
- 1 can (7 ounces) white or shoepeg corn, drained
- 1 can (16 ounces) vegetarian refried beans, warmed
- 1-1/2 cups shredded lettuce
- 1-1/2 cups shredded cheddar cheese
- 2 medium ripe avocados, peeled and sliced
- 1-1/2 cups chopped tomatoes
- 6 tablespoons sour cream

DIRECTIONS

1. In a large ungreased skillet, cook tortillas for 1-2 minutes on each side or until lightly browned. Remove and set aside.
2. In the same skillet, saute mushrooms and zucchini in oil until crisp-tender. Add salsa and corn; cook for 2-3 minutes or until heated through.
3. Spread refried beans over each tortilla; top with lettuce, salsa mixture, cheese, avocados, tomatoes and sour cream.

Nutritional Value: 343 calories | 25g protein. | 20g fat | 34g carbohydrate | Fiber: 26g

TWO-BEAN TOMATO BAKE

PREP TIME: 20 MINS   **COOK TIME:** 35 MINS   **SERVINGS:** 4

Dive into a wholesome and fiber-rich culinary experience with our Two-Bean Tomato Bake. This comforting dish combines the goodness of two different beans and the tangy flavors of tomatoes, creating a delightful, nutritious casserole that's as hearty as it is healthy. Perfect for those seeking a meal that's both satisfying and full of dietary fiber.

INGREDIENTS

- 1-1/2 pounds fresh green beans, cut into 2-inch pieces
- 1-1/2 pounds fresh wax beans, cut into 2-inch pieces
- 5 medium tomatoes, peeled and cubed
- 1/2 pounds fresh mushrooms, sliced
- 1 medium sweet onion, chopped
- 10 tablespoons butter, divided
- 1-1/2 teaspoons minced garlic, divided
- 1-1/2 teaspoons dried basil, divided
- 1-1/2 teaspoons dried oregano, divided
- 1 teaspoon salt
- 1-1/2 cups soft bread crumbs
- 1/3 cup grated Parmesan cheese

Nutritional Value: 351 calories | 21g protein. | 10g fat | 40g carbohydrate | Fiber: 25g

DIRECTIONS

1. Place beans in a large saucepan and cover with water; bring to a boil. Cook, uncovered, 8-10 minutes or until crisp-tender. Drain; add tomatoes and set aside.
2. In a large skillet, saute mushrooms and onion in 4 tablespoons butter until crisp-tender. Add 1 teaspoon garlic, 1 teaspoon basil, 1 teaspoon oregano and salt; cook 1 minute longer.
3. Add to the bean mixture; toss to coat. Spoon into a greased 3-qt. baking dish. Melt the remaining butter; toss with bread crumbs, cheese, and remaining garlic, basil and oregano. Sprinkle over bean mixture.
4. Cover and bake at 400° for 20 minutes. Uncover; bake 15 minutes longer or until golden brown.

RED POTATOES WITH BEANS

PREP TIME: 10 MINS   **COOK TIME:** 20 MINS   **SERVINGS:** 4

Savor the perfect combination of tender red potatoes and hearty beans in this wholesome dish. Packed with fiber, this recipe not only tantalizes your taste buds but also provides a nutritious boost.

INGREDIENTS

- 6 small red potatoes, cut into wedges
- 1-1/3 pounds fresh green beans, trimmed
- 1/2 cup chopped red onion
- 1/2 cup Italian salad dressing

DIRECTIONS

1. Place the potatoes in a large saucepan and cover with water. Bring to a boil. Reduce heat; cover and cook until tender, 10-15 minutes.
2. Meanwhile, place green beans and water to cover them in a 2-qt. microwave-safe dish.
3. Cover and microwave on high until tender, 6-8 minutes. Drain potatoes and beans; place in a bowl. Add onion and dressing; toss to coat.

Nutritional Value: 224 calories | 23g protein. | 15g fat | 28g carbohydrate | Fiber: 24g

BLACK BEAN PASTA

PREP TIME: 20 MINS **COOK TIME:** 30 MINS **SERVINGS:** 4

Black bean pasta is a type of alternative pasta made from black beans, often blended with other legumes or flours like chickpea flour or brown rice flour. It's a good source of plant-based protein and fiber, making it a nutritious option for those following vegetarian, vegan, or gluten-free diets. Black bean pasta can be cooked and used similarly to traditional pasta, but with a slightly different texture and subtle bean flavor.

INGREDIENTS

- 9 ounces uncooked whole wheat fettuccine
- 1 tablespoon olive oil
- 1-3/4 cups sliced baby portobello mushrooms
- 1 garlic clove, minced
- 1 can (15 ounces) black beans, rinsed and drained
- 1 can (14-1/2 ounces) diced tomatoes, undrained
- 1 teaspoon dried rosemary, crushed
- 1/2 teaspoon dried oregano
- 2 cups fresh baby spinach

DIRECTIONS

1. Cook fettuccine according to package directions. Meanwhile, in a large skillet, heat oil over medium-high heat.
2. Add mushrooms; cook and stir 4-6 minutes or until tender. Add garlic; cook 1 minute longer.
3. Stir in black beans, tomatoes, rosemary and oregano; heat through. Stir in spinach until wilted. Drain fettuccine; add to bean mixture and toss to combine.

Nutritional Value: 250calories | 25g protein. | 15g fat | 30g carbohydrate | Fiber: 24g

FARRO KALE SALAD

PREP TIME: 10 MINS   **COOK TIME:** 20 MINS   **SERVINGS:** 4

Delve into the goodness of our Farro Kale Salad, a vibrant medley of whole grains, fresh kale, and an array of delectable ingredients. This wholesome salad not only tantalizes your taste buds but also boasts an abundance of fiber to keep you feeling satisfied and nourished. It's a delightful combination of flavors and nutrients, making it the perfect choice for a wholesome meal.

INGREDIENTS

- 1 cup Farro
- 1 1/2 cup water
- 3 carrots cut into 1/2 inch pieces
- 1 cup cubed butternut squash
- 2 cups Brussels sprouts
- 1 TBS & 1 tsp olive oil
- 1/8 tsp salt
- 1/2 cup sliced almonds
- 3 Medjool dates seed removed and diced.
- 4 cups chopped kale
- 1/2 cup feta cheese crumbles

For the dressing:
- 1/3 cup olive oil
- 1/4 cup red wine vinegar
- 1 TBS Za'atar spice mix
- 2 tsp honey

DIRECTIONS

1. Bring water to a boil. Toss in Farro, stir, and reduce heat to the lowest setting and cook for 20 minutes.
2. Pour Farro into a colander to drain excess water. Let cool. Toss carrots, squash and Brussels sprouts in olive oil and spread out on a large baking sheet.
3. Sprinkle with salt. Place in a 500F oven and roast for 10 – 12 minutes until the Brussels sprouts begin to caramelize but not burn. In a large bowl massage kale until it is silky. Toss in Farro, roasted vegetables, almonds, and dates.
4. In a small bowl whisk together the dressing ingredients.
Pour dressing into salad and toss to coat. Sprinkle feta cheese over the top and serve.

Nutritional Value: 343 calories | 25g protein. | 23g fat | 30g carbohydrate | Fiber: 24g

SMOKY BEANS & BAKED EGGS

PREP TIME: 10 MINS   **COOK TIME:** 30 MINS   **SERVINGS:** 4

Start your day with a hearty and high-fiber breakfast by indulging in our Smoky Beans & Baked Eggs. This dish brings together the smoky goodness of beans with perfectly baked eggs, creating a protein-packed morning delight that keeps you energized and full of flavor. It's a nutritious and satisfying way to fuel your day.

INGREDIENTS

- 2 tbsp oil
- 1 onion, chopped
- 1 red pepper, sliced
- 3 garlic cloves, crushed
- 2 tsp smoked paprika
- 1 tbsp ketchup
- 400g can chopped tomatoes
- 2 x 400g cans black or pinto beans, drained
- 4-6 eggs, depending on how hungry you are (adults may want 2 eggs each)
- handful of coriander, leaves picked

DIRECTIONS

1. Heat the oil in a wide, shallow pan and cook the onion for 8-10 mins until softened. Add the pepper and cook for another 5 mins, stirring regularly, until softened.
2. Stir in the garlic, paprika and ketchup, then tip in the tomatoes, cover and leave to simmer gently for 10 mins.
3. Remove the lid and cook for a few more minutes to thicken, then add the beans. Can be cooled and frozen in portions at this stage.
4. Use a spoon to make 4-6 spaces in the mixture for the eggs – you should be able to see some of the bottom of the pan.
5. Crack the eggs one by one into a cup or bowl and gently drop one into each hole. Cover the pan and reduce the heat to low.
6. Cook for 3-5 mins until the egg whites are cooked through but the yolks are still runny. Scatter over the coriander to serve.

Nutritional Value: 344 calories | 25g protein. | 15g fat | 30g carbohydrate | Fiber: 25g

GRIDDLED CORNBREAD WITH DEVILLED EGGS & AVOCADO

PREP TIME: 5 MINS **COOK TIME:** 15 MINS **SERVINGS:** 2

Experience a delicious fusion of flavors and textures with this Griddled Cornbread, Deviled Eggs, and Avocado dish. Not only is it a treat for your taste buds, but it's also rich in fiber, making it a wholesome and satisfying meal. The crispy cornbread, creamy deviled eggs, and the buttery goodness of avocado come together for a delightful culinary adventure that will keep you energized and satisfied.

INGREDIENTS

- 400g can cherry tomatoes
- 1 tsp golden caster sugar
- a few drops Tabasco sauce
- 2 eggs
- ½ fat green chilli, thinly sliced (optional)
- small knob of butter, softened
- 1 small ripe avocado, halved, stoned, peeled and sliced (do this just before serving to prevent it from browning)
- 4 thick slices cornbread (see Goes Well with for recipe)
- handful coriander leaves, to serve

DIRECTIONS

1. Heat a griddle pan and a large frying pan. Put the tomatoes, sugar and Tabasco in the frying pan and bubble for 10 mins – season and taste to check the spiciness, adding a splash more Tabasco, if you like.
2. Make 2 spaces in the pan and crack in the eggs, then scatter over the chilli, if using. Cook for a further 3-5 mins until the whites of the eggs are cooked and the yolks are still runny (or to your liking).
3. Meanwhile, butter the cornbread and place, butter-side down, on the hot griddle pan. Cook for 2-3 mins each side until dark griddle lines appear.
4. Top the cornbread with the avocado and the eggs, then spoon around the tomatoes, scatter with coriander and serve.

Nutritional Value: 320 calories | 21g protein. | 12g fat | 30g carbohydrate | Fiber: 21g

CONCLUSION

As you reach the final page of "100 High Fiber Recipes," we want to express our heartfelt gratitude for embarking on this culinary journey with us. We hope that this cookbook has been a source of inspiration and a delicious guide to making fiber a fundamental part of your daily diet.

In a world where fast food and convenience often overshadow the importance of nutrition, "100 High Fiber Recipes" is here to remind you that eating well can be both delicious and satisfying. We believe in the power of food to nourish, heal, and bring joy, and it's our hope that the recipes you've discovered within these pages have allowed you to experience that power firsthand.

By incorporating the principles of a high-fiber diet into your daily routine, you're making an investment in your long-term health and well-being. Remember that your body deserves the best care, and this cookbook is a delicious and practical way to achieve that.

In closing, we encourage you to continue experimenting in the kitchen, exploring new flavors, and adapting these recipes to your personal tastes. We hope these recipes have encouraged you to see the incredible potential of high-fiber ingredients and have broadened your culinary horizons.

So, let's not say goodbye but rather, "See you at the next meal!" May your kitchen always be filled with the aromas of health, happiness, and the joy of creating nourishing dishes that you and your loved ones can savor together.

Thank you for choosing "100 High Fiber Recipes" to be your culinary companion. Wishing you a lifetime of good health, memorable meals, and the fulfillment that comes from savoring the goodness of a high-fiber, delicious life.

www.ingramcontent.com/pod-product-compliance
Lightning Source LLC
Chambersburg PA
CBHW042028150426
43198CB00003B/99